# Let's Bake Bread!

# Let's Bake Bread!

A Family Cookbook to Foster Learning,
Curiosity, and Skill Building in Your Kids

**BONNIE OHARA**

photography by Ashley Lima

Library of Congress Cataloging-in-Publication Data is on file.

ISBN 978-1-64829-057-2

Design by Ashley Lima

Artisan books are available at special discounts when purchased in bulk for premiums and sales promotions as well as for fundraising or educational use. Special editions or book excerpts can also be created to specification. For details, please contact special.markets@hbgusa.com.

The publisher is not responsible for websites (or their content) that are not owned by the publisher.

The Hachette Speakers Bureau provides a wide range of authors for speaking events. To find out more, go to hachettespeakersbureau.com or email HachetteSpeakers@hbgusa.com.

Published by Artisan,
an imprint of Workman Publishing Co., Inc.,
a subsidiary of Hachette Book Group, Inc.
1290 Avenue of the Americas
New York, NY 10104
artisanbooks.com

Artisan is a registered trademark of Workman Publishing Co., Inc., a subsidiary of Hachette Book Group, Inc.

Printed in China on responsibly sourced paper
First printing, September 2023

10 9 8 7 6 5 4 3 2 1

- - - - - - - - - - - - - - - - - - - -

This book is dedicated to my children, Sophia, Gabriel, and Leo. Baking and making a home and life with you are the memories we will keep long after you have grown into the amazing people you are bound to become. Working and learning alongside you has been the best of what life can be—humorous, artistic, thoughtful, philosophical, playful, creative, productive, meaningful.

I know one day I'll wish I could hear your small footsteps down the hall and see you appear in our kitchen with sleepy eyes and tousled hair, holding your blankets as I pull the bread from the oven. As I'm writing this, I would estimate I've got a few thousand more mornings just like that ahead of us. I'm so grateful for that, and for you.

 Mom

# Contents

# Preface

>>>>>>>>>>>>

Most Thursdays find me in the middle of everything, unloading golden loaves of sourdough from the stone deck ovens in my dining room, the early dawn light streaming across my workspace and casting amber beams through the room. I can see my eldest daughter snuggled up with a book on the couch, my youngest son fiddling with modeling clay in a pool of sunshine on the wood floor, and my middle child fussing with some origami. I work here, and so do they.

When my daughter Sophie was four years old, my son Gabriel was born, and I quit working outside the home so that I could care for my kids full-time. I began looking for ways to make up the difference of my lost income in my grocery budget. I started thinking about what common staples I could make myself. Eventually my scrutiny rested on the packaged loaves of sliced bread from the store. I relentlessly iterated my daily loaves, and while I worked, my kids would snuggle up with me on the kitchen floor, watching the bread rise through the oven window. That 45 minutes spent together, basking in the glow of warmth and oven light, was something special. I could almost feel the entire house sigh with enjoyment over a simple slice of warm bread.

As my sourdoughs began to refine into something resembling good bread, the kids and I fell deeply in love with the rhythm of baking and the routine it brought to our home life. They would often ask for a piece of dough to play with and mimic my hand movements as I worked. They would flip through cookbooks, looking for things to make, and request breads in all kinds of shapes. Suns and butterflies and snails sprinkled with poppy seeds. Flowers and leaves and turtles. Anything that captured our imagination, we tried to make.

Other bakers began to visit and bake with us, bringing with them bread and food traditions from all over the world. A visiting baker from Japan stayed for a week to bake shokupan. Our friend Ana came over to make pan de muerto. We hosted a Philadelphia pizzaiolo, pastry chefs from San Francisco and Los Angeles, and a baking instructor from Canada. We broadened our community and learned about human connection through bread.

Over time, our home has become a full-fledged cottage bakery where I turn out hundreds of loaves each week, all while homeschooling my kids. The crusty amber loaves pile up on wooden shelves as the timers are set and reset, oven load after oven load. I wear a path in the wood floor from the oven to the school table and back again, sometimes pausing to wave and exchange pleasantries with customers as they retrieve their still-warm loaves from the cabinet on my porch. Invariably a child appears, eager to show one of our regulars some small accomplishment—a Lego cat, an origami fox, a beautifully colored-in drawing, or a new phrase they learned in Japanese. Always they are met with earnest praise and friendly curiosity.

As the day wears on, more loaves will pass through my hands and out the door to our beloved customers and friends. I imagine the bread imbued with the poems read aloud, the stories of adventures, math computations, and all the sweet, silly, and important conversations my kids and I have shared. Folded into the dough are gravity and Galileo, the poetry of Emily Dickinson, and every sort of bird we can think of and how their nests are built, where they go in which season, and what seeds they eat. Are they the seeds that become our wheat, the wheat that becomes our bread? Each subject flows into the next.

Years of homeschooling and running a cottage bakery have become a daily balance that I call my "tiny bakery school." It seems to me that everything eventually somehow traces back to bread. From ancient civilizations and Greek myths to percentages and ratios, botany and biology, the seasons and communities, it's all bread to me.

# Baking Bread with Kids

Operating a small home bakery while homeschooling three kids has been my daily life for many years. I started out as a mom looking for economical ways to feed my family and eventually found a passion and expertise in baking bread. For years, I've offered baking classes in my home workspace on weekends. I've taught baking with our homeschool community, at local high schools, and with the 4H heirloom skills club, teaching every age from kindergartners to high school seniors and all kinds of mixed-age groups. I've loved watching concepts click for my students and seeing their satisfaction when they create a beautiful bread. I've loved that they've invested in something for themselves, spending an afternoon learning a skill they would get to keep forever.

Every subject and every lesson I've ever wanted to teach my children can be found in baking bread. We learn math while doubling, tripling, or halving recipes. We weigh and measure. We learn about temperatures and talk about the seasons. We learn about our food and develop a sense of locality. We ask questions and answer them using the scientific method; we run experiments side by side with changes in variables. We talk about the economy of the kitchen, how to save for what we need, and how to apply our skills. We travel the world by cooking through recipes we find in books and from our friends of other cultures. We gather wheat grown nearby and we mill it ourselves, turning it into flour right before our eyes. Bread gives us a glimpse into history and aligns us with peasants and farmers and scientists and revolutionaries and pioneers. Bread is mentioned in just about every old fairy tale and fable, illustrating the depth of its importance as a foundation of family, community, hearth, and home. We don't learn these things by rote; we live them.

# Why Bake Bread with Your Kids?

The primary goal of baking bread with kids is always somewhere in the middle of teaching, learning, and spending quality time with each other. No matter how your children are schooled or what your line of work is, all parents grapple with similar struggles—attempting to do some satisfying work, putting food on the table day after day, and somehow finding time to model important values and stay connected with their kids. Baking bread is an enjoyable activity that evokes so many of the lessons we try to impart to our young ones while reinforcing topics they might be covering in school, such as math, science, organization, and more. I would venture to say that baking a couple times a month with your kids will ignite curiosity, forge relationships with your local food producers and neighborhood, and help your children cultivate healthy connections to their food. Modeling critical thinking, community, creativity, and curiosity is a curriculum we all need, young and old.

Bread is a beautiful way to make learning fun—there is no need to force it. The most important learning moments can come from simple things like touching the butter, or stacking the bowls, or figuring out that you don't like basil. Sometimes, just letting kids show up authentically to a no-pressure activity is enough. It's unrealistic to think parents always have the energy to engage their kids in learning activities. But every time I say yes to kid participation in the kitchen, we end up having enriching interactions that make the little messes and extra time so worthwhile. The joy of pulling a warm loaf out of the oven might be enough to get your child excited about baking bread with you, but the following takeaways and lessons will keep you both coming back for more.

**Engage the Senses.** Sensory memories stick! Most of our beloved childhood memories come from moments when our senses were engaged—for example, touching a starfish at an aquarium (the cold water, the bumpy texture, the briny smell of the seawater) or making pancakes with a parent (the warmth of the stove, the heavenly scent of butter in the pan, the motion

of flipping a pancake). You don't have to do something every day, or every week, for it to become a solid core memory. Baking bread with kids once a month is enough to build a lifetime of quality memorable moments.

**Build Resilience.** Your baking projects will present many opportunities to model calmness in sticky situations, showing how we can push through feelings of uncertainty and learn from our mistakes. When we hear our children say things like "This is too hard" or "I can't do this," we can remind them of all the tricky things they have already mastered, and the effort they put in to get there. That feeling of accomplishment stays with us for a lifetime.

**Practice the Golden Rule.** We would all like to be treated with grace, patience, and gentle thoughtfulness. Encountering new situations in a low-risk environment like the home kitchen is a great way to model these skills. A dropped egg, spilled milk, or even an imperfect loaf of bread is not going to end the world; your calm and confident leadership will teach your children exactly how to behave when they find themselves in a challenging situation outside the home.

**Bond Without Materialism.** Baking a loaf of bread is a low-cost, nonmaterialistic way to spend time together. You can celebrate the seasons by making a flavorful bread, go on a walk to pick flowers and herbs to use in your dough, or celebrate a milestone by making your favorite recipe. Through the love and care you put into your bread, your family might start to think more about what they can make or do for others instead of what they can buy.

You must know that there is nothing more powerful, more meaningful, and more vital for development than warm memories, especially those of childhood, of home. We all value schooling but often forget that those good, sacred memories preserved from our youth were perhaps some of our best forms of education.

> "You are told a lot about your education, but some beautiful, sacred memory, preserved since childhood, is perhaps the best education of all. If a man carries many such memories into life with him, he is saved for the rest of his days. And even if only one good memory is left in our hearts, it may also be the instrument of our salvation one day."
>
> —FYODOR DOSTOYEVSKY

# How to Use This Book

While this book is meant to inspire parents and caretakers to bake with their children, the recipes are high quality and delicious for any age group. Adults, too, may learn a great deal about baking, with playful help from their kids. The recipes are organized into four chapters. Each chapter focuses on a theme or type of bread and contains lessons geared toward a particular age group. The recipes begin with the easiest, most approachable types of dough and work forward into more advanced recipes. All of the recipes include annotations that are developmentally appropriate for the key ages of each chapter. If you are working with kids of different ages, try the recipes in the first two chapters before attempting the later chapters. The foundational recipes are classic breads that someone of any age would benefit from knowing how to make.

No matter which recipes you choose, what level of baking experience you have, or how old your baking companions are, the following baking guidelines will support your time together in the kitchen.

**Get Organized.** Prepare your tools and ingredients before you begin to bake. If the child you are baking with is too young to weigh or measure ingredients, you may want to do all that weighing and measuring before inviting the child to join you. Having the right-size bowl, all your ingredients prepped, and the baking sheet ready will give you the mental space to work through the recipe together without distraction.

**Familiarize Yourself with the Recipes.** Always read through a recipe on your own before engaging your child, especially if they are on the young side. Reading instructions while a little one chats in your ear is a big challenge. To prepare, go over the recipe you plan to make and familiarize yourself with the basic steps and processes.

**Give Yourself Enough Time.** Try to pick a baking day that has ample free time, and remember that the time a dough needs for rising can change with the weather (see page 27). No one likes to realize that their bread is due to go in the oven at the same time

they need to run off for another obligation. Familiarizing yourself with what you'll be doing and making sure you have plenty of free time really helps keep the process fun and relaxed.

**Have Patience and Embrace Imperfection.** Yes, patience. Try to keep in mind that all messes can be cleaned up. If we stress about our kids cracking an egg "the wrong way," they will never learn to crack an egg. Failure has to be an option, and even encouraged, in the safe space of the home. Almost any baking mistake can be eaten or learned from.

**Find Your Rhythm.** Routines are a great comfort to children, and bread baking is a wonderful way to set one. Picking a particular day of the week to dedicate to your bread practice brings a rhythm to their schedule, with days that your child will look forward to. Whether it's Friday night pizza or Monday afternoon bread baking, these family traditions don't have to be grand to be cherished by everyone in the house.

**Make Room for Play.** Play is one of the best ways to engage young people in learning. If your kid wants to sculpt a pile of flour into a mountain range, poke a smiley face into their bread dough, or stretch their tiny breads into goofy shapes, encourage it. Even older kids like to goof around. Creating a playful environment keeps kids coming back for more fun baking time with the important grown-ups in their lives.

**Share in the Cleanup.** Baking is a wonderful way to gently teach children—whatever their age—how to clean up after themselves. Keep on hand a small dustpan with a brush for sweeping flour and crumbs off the countertops, along with a child-size broom. I quietly hand a damp rag to one of my kids when they make a small spill or hand them the tiny dustpan for their spilled flour. This isn't done punitively ("Messes are wrong and your punishment is cleaning it!") but helpfully ("It's okay to spill. Here's a towel!"). Your kids can wash bowls, dishes, and tools as well. The most effective way to clean dough from bowls, spoons, or counters is to scrape them off immediately with a plastic scraper while the dough is still soft. Kids can do this by themselves and usually find it pretty fun.

# Tools of the Trade

Baking is an affordable, minimalist practice and teaching tool. Plus, after any initial learning mishaps are out of the way, baking at home will save you a bit of money at the grocery store. While compared to, say, golf or violin lessons, the initial investment is quite low, but you do need a few tools to get started.

## The Basics

Before you get to baking, you'll want to make sure you own the following tools.

**Digital Scale** Once you use a scale to weigh ingredients for your recipes, you will never look back. If everyone in your household scooped a cup of flour and then weighed it, you'd find that each of those scoops has a slightly different weight, but on a scale, a gram is always a gram! Weighing ingredients on a digital scale is simple, and the improved accuracy will allow you to bake with much more consistent results.

**Digital Instant-Read Thermometer** Good bakers track their dough temperature. Read the section on why dough temperature is so important (page 196). To keep track of the temperature, use a quick and accurate digital thermometer. A waterproof one is great in case a young person drops it in the sink!

**Large Metal Bowls** Large steel bowls, able to hold 8 quarts (8 liters), can be found at restaurant supply stores and will allow you and your little ones to mix vigorously without your ingredients going astray. They are durable, will last a lifetime, and are a worthy investment if you want to bake bread regularly.

**Metal Half-Sheet Pans** Invest in a few high-quality 18 by 13-inch (43 by 31 cm) half-sheet pans that won't warp at high temperatures. Please don't use glass or ceramic bakeware, which can break, is heavy, and doesn't conduct heat well or hold up to high temperatures. My favorite half-sheet pan is made by USA Pan (see Resources, page 232).

**Parchment Paper** Parchment paper will keep your baking sheets in good condition and prevent sticking when you're making sweet bread recipes. Try parchment paper in precut sheets, which, unlike rolled parchment paper, will lay flat on the pan.

**Loaf Pans** You'll need a couple of standard-size loaf pans, which are called "9 by 5-inch" or "1-pound" pans, though they are not always exactly 9 by 5 inches nor do they hold exactly 1 pound of dough. Look for pans that are sturdy and conduct heat well—no glass or ceramic, please! My favorite is the medium loaf pan from USA Pan (see Resources, page 232), which measures 8.5 by 4.5 by 2.75 inches (23 by 13 by 6 cm) and has an excellent nonstick quality.

## Investment Pieces

These additional tools will help you tackle the more advanced recipes in this book.

**Pizza Stone** A decent pizza stone can cost between $40 and $50, which is probably the equivalent of one or two take-out pizza nights for a family with kids. I recommend getting the biggest pizza stone you can find in your price range because a larger surface makes landing pizzas less stressful. A pizza stone can also be used for baking bread, and keeping one in the oven can help regulate the oven's temperature.

**Dutch Oven** A cast-iron Dutch oven helps regulate the temperature in the oven and delivers a steamy heat to your loaf that vastly improves the crust. A 5-quart cast-iron Dutch oven from Lodge (see Resources, page 232) costs between $40 and $50, and if you plan on making quite a few sourdough boules, you'll appreciate the payoff.

**Proofing Baskets/Bannetons** You can certainly proof round hearth loaves in a colander lined with a kitchen towel and dusted with flour, and that will go just fine. But when you get serious about baking, you may want to invest in a couple of the cane or wicker baskets lined with linen that bakers use specifically for proofing bread. They are also called bannetons or sometimes brotforms, but if you're shopping online, a search for "proofing basket" should help you find what you need.

## Other Useful Kitchen Gear

The following tools are nice to have on hand, though not required.

• Plastic and/or metal dough scraper

• Rolling pin. I prefer a French rolling pin, which is a simple wooden pin without handles, but kids might prefer the handles for easier gripping.

• Whisk

• Pizza cutter

• Rubber spatula (to scrape out your bowls)

• Kid-friendly knife, such as an Opinel knife. They have a kids' section on their website with a variety of great choices that are affordable and have a rounded tip for kids but are still sharp enough to cut well. (Of course, always supervise children when they use a sharp knife.)

# Core Ingredients: Flour, Yeast, Salt, and Water

Before you begin baking, familiarize yourself with the ingredients. All bread recipes include flour; yeast or some other leavening agent, such as sourdough starter; salt; and water. Having an understanding of how your ingredients function will serve you well when working through the recipes. If you'll be baking with an older kid, make sure to read this section together!

## Flour

Bread is made from mostly flour, and while you can't tell from looking at those bags of flour on the shelves in the grocery store, flour comes from wheat. Wheat is a grass plant, and when it grows tall in the fields, it produces seeds at its top. The seeds are called "wheat berries," and they are the part of the plant that is harvested by farmers. You could put those seeds right back into the ground and grow more wheat, or, if you grind up the seeds, you make wheat flour.

Not all flours are created equal. For the recipes in this book, I recommend King Arthur All-Purpose Flour, which has a high protein content (this is a good quality for bread baking because it aids in strong gluten development), is widely available in grocery stores, and produces consistent results. While all the recipes in this book have been tested using King Arthur All-Purpose Flour, you can also substitute whole wheat flour if you'd prefer.

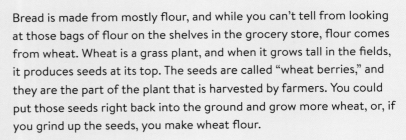

## BREAD FLOUR

New bakers often become curious about bread flour. Bread flour typically has a higher protein content than all-purpose flour, which means it absorbs more water and the gluten develops more quickly. When using bread flour, you might need to add a tiny bit more water to your dough and knead it a little bit less.

## WHOLE-GRAIN AND HEIRLOOM FLOURS

Working with local and heirloom whole-grain flours can require a little extra knowledge and expertise because the absorption rate and protein content of different types of flour can vary wildly from harvest to harvest, from season to season, and by how finely or coarsely a mill grinds the flour. These factors all play a major role in how recipes behave. By the time you have baked through this book, you will be a confident baker with great baking instincts, and you may feel comfortable working with whole-grain flours sourced from your local community.

# Yeast

Yeast is the leavening agent in bread; it makes bread rise and gives it a spongy texture. But what is it really? Yeast is a member of the fungus kingdom, the same group of organisms that includes mushrooms! Yeast is a single-celled living organism that can be found in the natural environment all around us—on the skins of grapes and other fruits, on grains, in flour, and in the air. Yeast eats carbohydrates and produces gas in a process called fermentation. If you've ever inspected a slice of bread, you've probably noticed that the texture is kind of like a sponge, filled with tiny air bubbles. Those air bubbles are made from gas produced by yeast.

All the recipes in this book were tested with Saf-instant Yeast (see Resources, page 232). Unlike other instant yeasts, Saf-instant doesn't need to be bloomed or proofed before being used for baking. Add it to the dough and it works every time!

## Salt

Salt gives bread its flavor and also improves its texture. You only need to forget the salt once to realize that bread's flavor and texture just aren't right without salt.

You can use almost any salt you already have for baking bread. Kosher salt, sea salt, and even Himalayan pink salt work just fine. The only important qualification is that the salt should be fine, not coarse, so it incorporates well into the bread dough.

## Water

Water hydrates the flour, forms the dough, and makes wheat more digestible. Getting the right ratio of water to flour is key for a successful bread. Too little water creates a stiff, dense dough that results in a dry, hard bread. Too much water creates a dough that is like mud or paste and results in a shapeless bread without much volume.

Different flours have different absorption rates, and even the weather can affect how your flour absorbs water. When you bake, take note of how your dough feels to the touch. Over time, you will come to learn by feel when you need to add or hold back a tiny bit of water to achieve a proper dough.

# Temperature and Time

Two very important elements in bread making are temperature and time. These two factors are interconnected: Dough that is too cold won't rise properly, while dough that is too hot can rise far too quickly. This happens because yeast does its best work within a temperature range of 75° and 80°F (24° and 27°C)—like a warm, but not too hot, sunny day. The active yeast inside the dough is blowing hundreds of tiny bubbles—faster in warm temperatures and slower in cool temperatures. However, the dough can take only so much air, and just like blowing a bubble with bubble gum, if the bubbles get too big, they will pop, and your bread will deflate! Mastering temperature and time is the real difference between simply following a recipe and becoming a good baker.

The best way to ensure your dough rises on time is to make sure the water (or other liquid ingredients) you use to make the dough is the correct temperature. For the most accurate numbers, advanced bakers and older kids can follow the temperature calculations on page 196. But beginners and little kids will want to refer to the chart at right as a shortcut, assuming that your flour is kept at room temperature. Water temperature can easily be adjusted by adding ice to cool it down or mixing lukewarm water with hot water from the tap.

| AIR AND FLOUR TEMPERATURE | WATER/LIQUID TEMPERATURE |
|---|---|
| 55 | 110 |
| 60 | 100 |
| 65 | 90 |
| 70 | 80 |
| 75 | 70 |
| 80 | 60 |
| 85 | 50 |
| 90 | 40 |

# How Bread Is Made

Unlike cooking, which involves an array of techniques and skills, baking is relatively straightforward and follows a predictable sequence. While at first the process may feel awkward and rife with questions (Am I doing this right? Is this dough the right consistency?), after a few tries you will find yourself in a familiar rhythm. Take the time to acquaint yourself with the basic flow of steps. Having an overall understanding of what happens at each step, and why, will give you a big-picture view of how bread comes together—and help ensure that the process goes smoothly for you.

## SCALING/MEASURING/ TEMPERATURE
*(Objective: Accuracy and preparation)*

Make sure you have all the ingredients you'll need, and in the correct amounts. Your main goal here is accuracy. Incorrect ratios of ingredients can result in dough that is too sticky or too dry or doesn't rise properly. Forgetting one of the few ingredients will leave you with inedible bread!

To measure, place a bowl on the scale, zero out the weight, then add one of the ingredients. When you have the right weight for that ingredient, set that bowl aside. Repeat this step with the other ingredients. For beginners and young children, it's best to use separate bowls for each ingredient; this way if there is a small spill with the salt or yeast, you can just spoon the excess out of the bowl—it won't be mixed with any other ingredients.

Be sure to get your water or liquid to the right temperature so the dough rises on a predictable timeline; see the chart on page 27.

## MIXING
*(Objective: Uniformly combined ingredients)*

A bread recipe typically has four to six main ingredients, and they all have a job to do. Properly mixing your ingredients ensures that they all make contact and can work together to create a perfect dough. When the recipe method dictates dispersing the yeast (or sourdough starter) into water, take your time. When combining the rest of the ingredients, be patient; you want to mix the dough until it begins to become smooth. Leaving dry bits of flour in your dough means having dry clumps of flour in your bread. Try setting a timer and mixing for five minutes.

## KNEADING OR FOLDING
### (Objective: Gluten development)

Kneading bread dough is a little bit like chewing gum! You take a soft dough and strengthen it by handling it a lot, which allows it to rise while holding a nice shape. You accomplish this by folding the dough repeatedly over and over itself. When you start, it will feel very soft and stretchy, but as you work the dough it will become bouncy and tight. This will give the dough a smooth appearance, and when it rises it will look like a beautiful round moon. If your dough ends up looking a bit scraggly, it may mean it wasn't kneaded very well or mixed well in the beginning.

## FIRST RISE OR FERMENTATION
### (Objective: Dough expansion)

After you've worked hard to weigh, mix, and knead, it's time to take a nice long break and let the yeast do some work. The fermentation time for the dough will depend on two factors: the quantity of yeast in the dough (more yeast rises faster, less yeast rises slower) and the dough temperature (warmer is faster, cooler is slower). Regardless of these factors, you want to see the dough expand.

The yeast will create little air pockets in the dough, and those air pockets create the desirable texture of bread and the flavor. Your only job during this phase is to allow your dough enough time to slowly blow up, like a balloon, but not so much time that it overinflates (pop!). Set a timer according to the recipe instructions, and put your dough in a spot that is not too hot and not too cold.

# SHAPING

*(Objective: Structure, functionality, and beauty)*

Shaping plays a critical role in giving breads their texture. You can make a pizza, a loaf of sandwich bread, or a dinner roll out of the exact same dough simply by shaping it in different ways. This is the part of baking that may feel a little strange or difficult at first, but your skill will improve with practice.

The goal of shaping is to create a symmetrical, even dough while preserving the air that has built up inside. This requires gentle handling. Remember: The air in the dough is an integral part of the flavor and texture that you will enjoy in your bread. If you press all those glorious bubbles out of your dough, you will end up with something like a brittle cracker instead of a nice airy crumb. Be careful to not tear the dough; making a roll or a loaf that can rise high means preserving the surface tension of the dough.

All that said, playing around with your dough is just fine and having fun is an invaluable part of the process. With very little kids, perfection isn't a priority over fun, but older kids will want to do their best work and handle their dough with more delicacy.

## 6

### FINAL PROOF

*(Objective: Volume/height and flavor)*

After the loaf has taken its shape, you will place it in a loaf pan or a basket to rest and have its final rise, or "proof." In this step, the fermentation is doing the work again; your job is to set a timer and get your oven ready. The dough will grow a final time and develop more flavor and air bubbles.

As with the first rise (step 4), timing is key. Dough baked too soon will be smaller in size and have a less fluffy interior texture. Dough that rises too long will pop and deflate. Knowing when your dough is perfectly proofed takes practice. A nicely proofed loaf feels a bit like a marshmallow—it's airy and very soft, but it still bounces back a little bit when pressed.

## 7

### BAKING

*(Objective: Evenly baked bread)*

You want an even bake with a beautiful bronze color on your bread. The first few times you tackle any recipe, you should check on your bread often, starting at about halfway through the full baking time. Every home oven is a little different, and part of getting good at baking is getting good at knowing your oven. Some are hotter from the bottom, others from the top, and baked goods need to be moved closer or farther away from an aggressive heating element. Some ovens have a hot back corner, and baked goods need to be pulled toward the front or rotated halfway through the baking time. And if you accidentally burn a loaf while you're still getting familiar with your oven's specific temperatures, just know that it happens and it's totally okay.

## 8

### COOLING

*(Objective: A set crust and crumb)*

Letting your bread cool allows the crust and crumb to set for easier slicing. Nevertheless, there are few pleasures in life as fine as ripping into a warm loaf of bread and inhaling the steam that rises from it. So sometimes, you might choose to skip this step and enjoy your bread while it's still warm.

If you plan to store your loaf, let it cool completely on a wire rack first. Putting a hot loaf directly into a paper or plastic bag will cause it to steam inside the bag, leaving you with a soft and possibly soggy crust. Slicing your loaf before bagging it can make it easier to store, and more convenient for kids to help themselves to it.

# Storing Bread

If your bread is soft and squishy, and needs to stay that way, storing it in a resealable plastic bag is the best option. If your bread is supposed to have a crispy crust, a paper bag will allow airflow and let your crust stay crunchy a little bit longer. In either case, your homemade bread lacks the preservatives that are used in commercial breads, so it should be stored at room temperature only for four to six days or so.

If you need to prolong the life of your homemade bread, slice it, place it inside a resealable plastic freezer bag, and freeze the sliced loaf. Now you can pull out the bread one slice at a time and defrost it in a toaster or a skillet.

One other way to store bread is with a beeswax food wrap (see Resources, page 232). Similar to a paper bag, beeswax food wrap protects the bread from drying out but still allows it to breathe. Plus it is washable, reusable, and eco-friendly.

# Enriched Breads for Beginners

RECIPES TO ENGAGE THE SENSES, FOR AGES 3 TO 7

## In This Chapter

Embark on your baking adventures with dough in the simplest form: cloud bread, a soft, fluffy, bouncy bread with a light, airy interior and subtle sweetness. It's a wonderful project for beginner bakers and children, as the dough is nearly foolproof. The basic dough recipe (page 43) includes lots of extra reassurance and tips for baking with small kids. The recipes that follow are variations on that basic dough, each one including age-appropriate cues, learning moments, and conversation starters.

Cloud dough is a soft, simple enriched dough. "Enriched" means the dough includes fat (like oil, butter, or eggs) and sometimes a sweetener (like honey, agave, maple syrup, molasses, or sugar). These ingredients have a softening effect on the dough, which makes enriched doughs fun to work with and forgiving. Enriched doughs can handle a bit of extra kneading and handling, which smaller kids and beginner bakers alike love to do!

Making the basic cloud bread dough teaches the hand skills needed to bake bread (mixing, kneading, and shaping). Then, as kids gain confidence, they can try making shapes like Herbed Leaf, Snail, and Flower Rolls (page 47) or Sweet Dreams Bunny Bread (page 63), and they can incorporate new ingredients with the Winter Warming Spices Bread (page 66), and have fun playing with colors while making Cookie Bread (page 73) or Springtime Tie-Dye or Rainbow Bread (page 76).

# Learning Opportunities

Baking, playing, and having fun are all, in themselves, forms of learning, so don't feel pressured to make every moment of the bread-making process teachable or educational. Enjoy the time together and rest assured: Sweet teachable moments such as these will be a natural by-product of baking time.

### Fine Motor Skills

As they pick and pluck herbs, run their hands through bowls of seeds, and squish and shape dough, children develop fine motor skills. Strengthening hands through pinching, grabbing, and squeezing prepares kids for holding and manipulating tools of all kinds, from pencils to forks to shoelaces.

### Sensory Awareness

Young kids can use baking to discover the connection between the mind and body. Adults, as guides, can help kids connect their tactile senses to their thoughts and feelings. Take time along the way to ask what they feel, smell, touch, hear, and taste, and then talk about it. Do you feel the warmth from the oven? Do you smell the bread baking? What sound do you hear when you tap on the finished bread? What flavors do you taste in this, and what do they remind you of?

### Structure and Predictability

Incorporating bread baking into a weekly routine has myriad benefits. Little ones love predictability, and knowing that a particular day brings the promise of warm bread and cozy connection defines the week nicely for them. When my kids see a baking project unfolding in the kitchen, they can't be stopped from bringing over a stool and getting involved as quickly as possible. Nurturing that peaceful and playful environment will ensure that your kids do the same.

# Baking with Your Senses

Bread baking is full of sensory stimulation, which makes it particularly well suited for young children. In fact, the best way to master bread baking is by letting your five senses guide you. Over time, with practice and patience, you will develop and refine your intuition and judgment, and your technique will improve. It's okay if the process feels a little awkward or the result isn't perfect. Just like everything else we learn to do (write our names, ride a bike, play an instrument), our careful attention and mindful practice will help us grow our skills.

## 1

### SIGHT

Visual cues are a strong indicator of how your dough is developing. Take notice of how the risen dough domes in the bowl or how the smooth surface develops tiny bubbles. See the way the dough changes color as it bakes, moving from pale to gold to tan. Watching for subtle changes and making sense of what you notice is an invaluable skill for bakers and one that parents can easily engage children in.

## 2

### TOUCH

Touch might be our most important sense for baking. Your hands can tell you how strong your dough is, whether it's too wet or too dry, and when you need to incorporate more water or flour to adjust. Does it stretch in your hands, or does it tear apart? Is it well mixed and soft, or is it dry and pebbled with unincorporated ingredients? As the dough rises, press it gently. Does it feel taut and bounce right back, or does it feel pillowy and soft? Eventually you will know the feeling of a perfectly proofed loaf just by touching it gently.

### 3
### SMELL

Bread and dough have a subtle aroma that changes over time. Take notice of how the dough smells when you first mix it, and how that scent evolves as the dough rises. When you are a beginner baker, it's a great practice to stay near your oven and pay attention to the changes in the scent of your baking loaf as it expands in the oven, as the crust sets, and as it finishes baking. In time, you will find yourself wandering over to the oven exactly one minute before the timer goes off because you can smell from across the house that your bread has finished baking.

### 4
### SOUND

Can you hear dough? Does it make a noise when it comes away from the sides of the bowl as you mix? Can you hear the delicate Bubble Wrap sound of interior air pockets popping when you shape it? Do your hands make a noise when brushing against a dusting of flour on the table? Can you hear the crackle of fresh bread coming out of the oven and meeting the cold air? When you tap or knock on the bottom of a finished crusty loaf, do you hear a hollow thump? All these sounds will help guide you in creating a perfect loaf.

### 5
### TASTE

The final and most wonderful part of baking is tasting. Tasting simply for joy should be your first priority. After you've done that, you can also taste critically. How is the flavor of the crust? Would it be better if it had been baked a bit darker or a bit lighter? How is the flavor of the crumb (the inside of the bread)? Neutral? Yeasty? Bitter or sour? Bread can develop flavors that are "off" if the dough is under- or over-proofed. How is the texture of the bread? Light and airy? Or dense and coarse? You can turn your thoughtful attention to the flavor and texture of your bread and make mental notes on how you would do things differently next time, or just fully appreciate the great work you've done and enjoy eating your bread!

# Cloud Bread Dough

This dough is the foundation for all the breads in this chapter. As you and your children work through the chapter, you will infuse the dough with different flavors and textures. Sensory details are part of the magic of bread baking, and the soft and bouncy texture of cloud bread dough makes it ideal for toddler- to kindergarten-age children to play with. Given how easy and fun it is to work with this dough, you may be surprised how beautiful the flavor of this bread is, with its subtle sweetness and tender texture.

*Makes 1 loaf or 8 to 10 rolls*

| INGREDIENT | WEIGHT | VOLUME |
| --- | --- | --- |
| Water | 260 g | 1 cup plus 2 tablespoons |
| Instant yeast | 12 g | 1 rounded tablespoon |
| All-purpose flour | 500 g | 4 cups |
| Honey (or any liquid sweetener you like) | 60 g | 3 tablespoons |
| Canola oil or other neutral oil | 50 g | ¼ cup |
| Fine salt | 10 g | 1½ teaspoons |
| Egg (optional, for egg wash) | | 1 |

**Prepare:** Temperature is an important consideration in baking. To keep your dough on the same timeline as this recipe, you will want to use the temperature chart (see page 27) to warm your liquid ingredients to the correct temperature. The chart is meant to be helpful, not something to worry about. Keep in mind that on cooler days (below 75°F/23°C) the dough may take a bit longer to rise. On warmer days (above 75°F/23°C) the dough may rise more quickly. This is still okay; just be mindful of it and try to get as close as possible to the target temperature. Weigh or measure all of your ingredients and gather your supplies.

 Little ones may have difficulty helping with the weighing, but if you have the patience for it, you can always start a conversation about the numbers on the scale with no pressure for them to perform; just ask if they see a favorite number that they recognize on the scale.

**Mix:** In a large bowl, dissolve the yeast into the water using a swishing motion with your hands.

Next, add the flour, honey, oil, and salt.

At this point, you and your helper can mix the dough by squishing the ingredients together with a grabbing hand motion. I use the cue "grab and squish" for mixing with kids. You can hold the bowl for kids if they want to do it "all by themselves." A more tentative child may look to you for

 "We're making a bubble bath," I often say as we swish the yeast and it creates gentle bubbles.

## cloud bread dough, continued

If mixing with a wooden spoon, sing "Row, Row, Row Your Boat" as you mix the dough until it is combined.

Sift a light dusting of flour over your child's palms and have them rub the flour between their hands. This will help them stay unstuck when they get their hands in the dough, without incorporating too much extra flour into the dough. You can do this as often as necessary.

encouragement and guidance; hold the bowl with one hand and join them in the squishing, your hand side by side with theirs. If your child is resistant to having messy hands, use a wooden spoon to combine the ingredients. Hold the bowl with both hands and teach your child to hold the spoon as if it were an oar. Have them grip the spoon with both hands and "row" toward themselves.

**Knead:** When your dough has come together into a shaggy mass, turn the dough out onto a lightly floured work surface. Using clean hands, knead the dough with a push-and-fold motion. Firmly push the dough away from you, then fold it back toward you, rotating the dough a quarter turn every few folds. Repeat pushing and folding for about 5 minutes, or until the dough feels smooth, tight, and bouncy.

**Rise:** Return the dough to the bowl. To prevent the dough from drying out, cover it with a kitchen towel (or plastic wrap, if necessary, in drier climates), and let rise for 90 minutes. Alternatively, you can use a reusable beeswax food wrap (see Resources, page 232). The dough should roughly double in size.

**Shape:** You can shape the dough into a sandwich loaf or into small rolls in creative shapes.

**To shape a loaf:** Turn the dough out onto a lightly floured work surface. Gently pat the dough out into a rough rectangle shape. Fold in the corners farthest from you as if you were folding in the sleeves of a T-shirt, then roll the dough up toward you like a yoga mat. Place it in a 9 by 5-inch (23 by 13 by 6 cm) loaf pan with the seam side down.

**To make rolls:** Line a sheet pan with parchment paper. Turn the dough out onto a lightly floured work surface. Divide the dough into 8 to 10 pieces, roughly 90 grams each. Shape each piece by covering it with a cupped hand and gently rounding it into a ball shape by pulling in a circular motion with your hands. You can leave the rolls in rounds or you can be creative, using small pieces of dough to enhance the shape, like you would with molding clay. We make turtles, snails, frogs, sticks, bones, ladybugs, leaves, and anything else we can dream up. Place the finished shapes on the prepared sheet pan, leaving a few inches between each one.

**Proof:** This is the final rise. Let the dough proof, uncovered, at room temperature in the loaf pan or on the sheet pan. A fully proofed loaf should rise above the edges of the pan and leave a soft impression when you press on it; this can take 45 minutes to an hour or more. With small rolls and shapes, 30 to 45 minutes at room temperature should be plenty to give them a soft, airy interior.

**Brush with Egg Wash:** If you want a shiny finish, you can apply an egg wash. Beat the egg with a fork in a small bowl and brush the loaf or each roll with the egg wash after proofing.

**Preheat:** While the dough is proofing, preheat the oven to 375°F (190°C).

**Bake:** Bake the loaf for 35 to 40 minutes, or bake the rolls for 18 to 20 minutes, until light golden brown. Peek halfway through the bake time and rotate the pan for a more even bake. Check the rolls on the early side to ensure they don't overbake.

**Cool:** An adult with oven mitts should unmold the loaf from the pan right away and transfer to a wire rack to let cool for at least 30 minutes; leaving it in the pan can steam the sides of the loaf, making it too soft and difficult to slice. Let the small rolls cool on the sheet pan for at least 20 minutes so the interior crumb can set and the breads can be safely handled.

Small breads tend to go stale quickly, so they are best when eaten within 2 days. Store them in a resealable plastic bag to keep them soft. For a loaf, slice before storing in a resealable plastic bag for up to 2 days.

Kids will want to play with their creations and show them off before devouring them. You can serve them with butter or jam and let the little ones enjoy their freshly baked bread!

# Herbed Leaf, Snail, and Flower Rolls

The leaf, snail, or flower shapes of these rolls can easily be made (and devoured!) by young children in the scope of an afternoon, but the flavor of the bread is sophisticated enough to serve to dinner guests—in which case, simply shape the dough into dinner rolls and brush them all over with melted garlic herb butter. Letting kids pick and pluck the leafy herbs is a great way for them to use their hands and practice their fine motor skills.

*Makes 8 to 10 leaf or snail rolls or pull-apart flower rolls*

| INGREDIENT | WEIGHT | VOLUME |
|---|---|---|
| Water | 290 g | 1¼ cups |
| Olive oil | 50 g | ¼ cup |
| Honey (or any liquid sweetener you like) | 20 g | 1 tablespoon |
| Instant yeast | 12 g | 1 rounded tablespoon |
| All-purpose flour | 400 g | 3⅓ cups |
| Whole wheat flour | 100 g | ¾ cup plus 2 tablespoons |
| Fresh herbs, such as parsley, thyme, chives, basil, or tarragon, chopped | | ⅓ cup (more or less herbs will not make or break this recipe; use what you have and what you like) |
| Fine salt | 10 g | 1½ teaspoons |
| **For the Garlic Herb Butter (optional):** | | |
| Unsalted butter, at room temperature | 60 g | 4 tablespoons |
| Garlic, crushed | | 1 clove |
| Fresh herbs, chopped | | 1 tablespoon |

**Prepare:** Use the temperature chart (see page 27) to prepare the water to the correct temperature. Keep in mind that on cooler days (below 75°F/23°C) the dough may take a bit longer to rise. On warmer days (above 75°F/23°C) the dough may rise more quickly. Weigh or measure all the ingredients and gather your supplies.

**Mix:** In a large bowl, combine the water, olive oil, honey, and yeast. Use a spoon to mix gently until the yeast is dispersed. Add the flours, herbs, and salt. Mix by hand, using a grab-and-squish motion to thoroughly combine all the ingredients. Alternatively, use a wooden spoon to mix. The dough is well mixed when it is smooth and there are no dry bits of flour. This may take about 5 minutes.

**Rest:** Cover the bowl with a kitchen towel and set aside to let the dough rest, relax, and rehydrate for 15 minutes.

**Knead:** Turn the dough out onto a lightly floured work surface. Knead the dough with a push-and-fold motion. Firmly push the dough away from you, then fold it back toward you, rotating the dough a quarter turn every few folds. Repeat pushing and folding for about 5 minutes, or until the dough feels smooth, tight, and bouncy.

**Rise:** Return the dough to the bowl, cover it with a kitchen towel (or plastic wrap, if necessary, in drier climates), and let rise for 90 minutes. The dough should roughly double in size.

continued

Have your little ones recognize that the shape of our hands and veins resembles that of leaves. Those veins bring nutrients to the leaves in the same way ours do!

Spirals are a fascinating shape in nature. Once you start to notice them, you will see them everywhere! Ask your child how many spirals they can think of or imagine. Snails, seashells, nautiluses, and many leaves and flowers unfurl from a spiral shape.

**Divide and Shape:** Line a sheet pan with parchment paper. Turn the dough out onto a lightly floured work surface. Divide the dough into 8 to 10 pieces, roughly 80 grams each.

**To make leaves:** Use your hands to gently flatten each piece into a leaf shape. Use a butter knife to press hard into the dough to create the veins in the leaves. Place the finished shapes on the prepared sheet pan, leaving a few inches between each leaf.

**To make snails:** Use your hands to roll each piece of dough into a long strand, then roll up the strand from one end to create a spiral. Using a butter knife or scissors, cut the end of the spiraled dough and use the cutting to make the snail antennae. Place the finished snail shapes on the prepared sheet pan, leaving a few inches between each snail.

**To make flower-shaped pull-apart rolls:** Use your hands to gently round each piece into a roll. Place one roll in the center of a 9-inch (22 cm) pie pan, then add as many rolls as you can fit into a circle around the center to make the flower (I usually use 5 or 6). You should have 1 or 2 rolls left over. Shape these into leaves and tuck them into the sides of the pie plate under the "flower petals."

**Proof:** Let the dough proof, uncovered, at room temperature on the sheet pan or in the pie pan for 30 to 45 minutes before baking.

**Preheat:** While the leaves, snails, or flower rolls are proofing, preheat the oven to 375°F (190°C).

**Make the Garlic Herb Butter:** If desired, in a small saucepan over low heat, gently warm the butter with the garlic and herbs until the butter has melted. Set aside.

**Bake:** Bake for 18 to 25 minutes, until the rolls are golden brown. Peek halfway through the bake time and rotate the pan for a more even bake. Check the rolls on the early side to ensure they don't overbake.

**Brush with Garlic Herb Butter:** If using, brush the rolls all over with the garlic herb butter just after baking.

**Cool:** Let the rolls cool on the sheet pan for about 15 minutes.

Small breads tend to go stale quickly, so they are best when eaten within 2 days. Store them in a resealable plastic bag to keep them soft.

## leaf rubbings

During the rise time, make leaf rubbings. Gather a few different types of tree leaves in various shapes and sizes. You'll also need crayons and drawing paper. Remove the wrappers from the crayons. Using tape, affix the leaves to the underside of the drawing paper. Rub the side of a crayon gently on the paper over the leaf. As you do this, you'll see the colored areas start to take the shape of the leaf.

This activity will help little ones feel the veins in the leaves, which is valuable tactile information. Tape the finished work to a window and watch the afternoon sun glow through the leaf rubbings. Let the leaf shapes inspire the leaves you make with the dough.

# On the Run Energy Buns (Flax, Chia, and Sesame Bread)

Seeds are a high-quality energy source for active kids. This recipe for energy buns is a great alternative to granola bars, with much more protein and a lot less sticky sugar. You can also shape the dough into a loaf for a fantastic morning or afternoon piece of toast with almond butter. Kids will enjoy mixing, kneading, and shaping this wonderfully textured and bumpy dough the same way they love running their hands through pebbles in a stream.

Makes 8 buns or 1 loaf

| INGREDIENT | WEIGHT | VOLUME |
|---|---|---|
| Flaxseed | 10 g | 1 tablespoon |
| Chia seeds | 10 g | 1 rounded tablespoon |
| Sesame seeds | 10 g | 1 tablespoon |
| Hot water | 40 g | ¼ cup plus 1 tablespoon |
| Water | 260 g | 1 cup plus 2 tablespoons |
| Honey (or any liquid sweetener you like) | 30 g | 1 rounded tablespoon |
| Canola oil or other neutral oil | 30 g | 2 tablespoons |
| Instant yeast | 12 g | 1 rounded tablespoon |
| All-purpose flour | 320 g | 2⅔ cups |
| Whole wheat flour | 100 g | ¾ cup plus 2 tablespoons |
| Fine salt | 6 g | 1 teaspoon |
| Egg (optional, for egg wash) | | 1 |

**Prepare:** Use the temperature chart (see page 27) to prepare the water to the correct temperature. Keep in mind that on cooler days (below 75°F/23°C) the dough may take a bit longer to rise. On warmer days (above 75°F/23°C) the dough may rise more quickly. Weigh or measure all the ingredients and gather your supplies.

**Make the Seed Mixture:** In a bowl, combine the seeds and cover with the hot water. Since seeds soak up a lot of water, they need to be soaked before you add them to the dough so they don't dry it out. The seeds typically need about 20 minutes to soak, which is plenty of time to get the other ingredients ready.

 Seeds in a large container can provide a tactile wonderland for kids to run their hands through. This is the type of sensory activity occupational therapists often provide to promote fine motor skills.

**Mix:** In a large bowl, combine the water, honey, oil, and yeast. Use a spoon to mix gently until the yeast is dispersed. Add the flours, salt, and seeds. Mix by hand, using a grab-and-squish motion to thoroughly combine all the ingredients. Alternatively, use a wooden spoon to mix. The dough is well mixed when it is smooth and there are no dry bits of flour. This may take about 5 minutes.

continued

Don't forget to engage your child as you work! Try asking, Doesn't that dough feel soft? Can you smell the yeast? Does that honey taste good? Can you hear your hands brushing against the table when you shape the dough?

**Rest:** Cover the bowl with a kitchen towel and set aside to let the dough rest, relax, and rehydrate for 15 minutes.

**Knead:** Turn the dough out onto a lightly floured work surface. Knead the dough with a push-and-fold motion. Firmly push the dough away from you, then fold it back toward you, rotating the dough a quarter turn every few folds. Repeat pushing and folding for about 5 minutes, or until the dough feels smooth, tight, and bouncy.

**Rise:** Return the dough to the bowl, cover it with a kitchen towel (or plastic wrap, if necessary, in drier climates), and let rise for 90 minutes. The dough should roughly double in size.

**Shape:**

**To shape buns:** Line a sheet pan with parchment paper. Turn the dough out onto a lightly floured work surface. Divide the dough into 8 golf ball–size pieces, roughly 100 grams each. To form the dough into buns, use your hands to gently round each piece. Place the buns on the prepared sheet pan, leaving a few inches between each bun.

**To shape a loaf:** Turn the dough out onto a lightly floured work surface. Gently pat the dough out into a rough rectangle shape. Fold in the corners farthest from you to meet in the middle, as if you were folding in the sleeves of a T-shirt, then roll the dough up toward you like a yoga mat. Place it in a 9 by 5-inch (23 by 13 by 6 cm) loaf pan with the seam side down.

**Proof:** Let the dough proof, uncovered, at room temperature on the sheet pan or in the loaf pan for 45 minutes before baking. If you are making a loaf, it may take over an hour. A fully proofed loaf should rise above the edges of the pan and leave a soft impression when you press it. The rolls will slightly enlarge and feel soft and airy when pressed.

**Preheat:** While the rolls or loaf are proofing, preheat the oven to 375°F (190°C).

**Brush with Egg Wash:** If desired, beat the egg with a fork in a small bowl and brush each roll or the loaf with the egg wash after proofing. This will give the bread a shiny appearance. You can also sprinkle some (unsoaked) seeds on top after egg washing if you like.

**Bake:** Bake the rolls for 18 to 20 minutes, or bake the loaf for 25 to 30 minutes, until golden brown. Peek halfway through the bake time and rotate the pan for a more even bake. Check the rolls on the early side to ensure they don't overbake.

**Cool:** Let the rolls cool on the sheet pan for about 15 minutes. An adult with oven mitts should unmold the loaf from the pan right away and transfer to a wire rack to let cool for 30 minutes; leaving it in the pan can steam the sides of the loaf, making it too soft and difficult to slice.

Small breads tend to go stale quickly, so they are best when eaten within 2 days. Store them in a resealable plastic bag to keep them soft. For a loaf, slice before storing in a resealable plastic bag for up to 5 days.

Let your small person peer over your shoulder and check when the rolls are done, too.

>>> turn the page for a yummy almond butter recipe!

## >>> Almond Butter

Almond butter is a great treat to make while this bread is baking. You can make almond butter from raw almonds, but I prefer the flavor of roasted. Roast the almonds while you are soaking the seeds for the bread and leave them to soak side by side. A bit of honey or cinnamon to taste is a welcome addition to almond butter, but it's perfectly good plain, too.

Makes about 3 cups (850 g)

| INGREDIENT | WEIGHT | VOLUME |
|---|---|---|
| Raw almonds | 400 g | 2⅔ cups |
| Boiling water | 400 g | 1⅔ cups |
| Kosher salt | 10 g | 2 teaspoons |
| Canola oil or other neutral oil | up to 39 g | 1 tablespoon at a time, as needed |
| Honey (or any liquid sweetener you like; optional) | | |

Let your young person spread the almonds on the baking sheet with their hands. Let them snack on a few (cooled) roasted almonds and compare the flavor to that of unroasted ones.

Let your child press the button on the blender or food processor and ask them if they can tell by the sound when the almond butter is smooth. Have them taste from a spoon and decide if they want the texture creamier or left chunkier, and if they want to add sweetener or leave it out.

Place the almonds in a medium heatproof bowl. Pour the boiling water over the almonds, add the salt, and stir gently to dissolve. Soak for 30 minutes.

Preheat the oven to 375°F (190°C).

Drain the almonds completely and discard the water. Spread the almonds on a baking sheet, then roast for 8 to 10 minutes, checking on the early side to ensure they don't overbake. They will be the color of brown kraft paper when finished and smell toasty.

**Cool:** Let the almonds cool on the baking sheet before processing, about 20 minutes.

**Blend:** In a blender or a food processor, process the cooled almonds for about 2 minutes, or until smooth and creamy. You'll likely need to stop the blender and use a rubber spatula to scrape down the sides a few times. If needed, stream in a small amount of oil, 1 tablespoon at a time, to reach a spreadable consistency. You shouldn't need more than 3 tablespoons of oil to bring the butter together (this depends on the age and moisture of the almonds, so it can vary). If desired, add honey to taste.

Store the almond butter in an airtight mason jar for up to 2 weeks at room temperature (refrigerating can make it impossible to stir).

# Fluffy French Milk Bread

These soft, buttery rolls, or pains au lait ("milk breads"), are a favorite after-school snack of children in France. The rolls can be made plain, but the most fun way to enjoy them is warm, with a cache of chocolate chips buried inside. My kids and I like to use milk chocolate for this recipe, but any chocolate that you and your kids like will work.

*Makes 10 rolls or 1 loaf*

| INGREDIENT | WEIGHT | VOLUME |
|---|---|---|
| Whole milk | 250 g | 1 cup plus 2 teaspoons |
| Sugar | 70 g | ⅓ cup |
| Unsalted butter, melted and cooled | 60 g | 4 tablespoons |
| Instant yeast | 12 g | 1 rounded tablespoon |
| All-purpose flour | 500 g | 4 cups |
| Fine salt | 8 g | 1 rounded teaspoon |
| Chocolate chips, or 2 milk chocolate bars, chopped (optional) | roughly 100 g | ⅔ cup |
| Egg (optional, for egg wash) | | 1 |

**Prepare:** Use the temperature chart (see page 27) to prepare the milk to the correct temperature. Keep in mind that on cooler days (below 75°F/23°C) the dough may take a bit longer to rise. On warmer days (above 75°F/23°C) the dough may rise more quickly. Weigh or measure all the ingredients and gather your supplies.

**Mix:** In a large bowl, combine the milk, sugar, butter, and yeast. Use a spoon to mix gently until the yeast is dispersed. Add the flour and salt. Mix by hand, using a grab-and-squish motion to thoroughly combine all the ingredients. Alternatively, use a wooden spoon to mix. The dough is well mixed when it is smooth and there are no dry bits of flour. This may take about 5 minutes.

**Rest:** Cover the bowl with a kitchen towel and set aside to let the dough rest, relax, and rehydrate for 15 minutes.

**Knead:** Turn the dough out onto a lightly floured work surface. Knead the dough with a push-and-fold motion. Firmly push the dough away from you, then fold it back toward you, rotating the dough a quarter turn every few folds. Repeat pushing and folding for about 5 minutes, or until the dough feels smooth, tight, and bouncy.

**Rise:** Return the dough to the bowl, cover it with a kitchen towel (or plastic wrap, if necessary, in drier climates), and let rise for 90 minutes.

continued

Dough with butter inside of it is more sensitive to cool temperatures. If the dough gets too cool during the rise time, the butter will become solid and the dough won't be able to rise. If your environment is a little chilly, you can make a proofing chamber for your dough. Place the dough in a closed, turned-off oven with the light on and set a pan of boiling water on the shelf underneath it. This will provide the gentle, steamy heat needed to rise the dough. The steaming water also prevents the dough from drying out since cold air is also typically very dry.

**Shape:**

**To shape rolls:** Line a sheet pan with parchment paper. Turn the dough out onto a lightly floured surface. Divide the dough into 10 pieces, roughly 70 grams each. To shape, flatten each piece of dough with your fingers and sprinkle chocolate chips or place a piece of a chocolate bar in the middle of the dough, then roll the dough up like a tiny yoga mat. You will end up with oblong rolls shaped like hot dog buns. Place the rolls spaced 2 inches (5 cm) apart on the prepared sheet pan.

**To shape a loaf:** Turn the dough out onto a lightly floured work surface. Gently pat the dough into a rough square shape. Sprinkle chocolate pieces all over the dough. Fold in the corners farthest from you to meet in the middle, as if you were folding in the sleeves of a T-shirt, then roll the dough up toward you like a yoga mat. Place it in a 9 by 5-inch (23 by 13 by 6 cm) loaf pan with the seam side down.

**Proof:** Let the dough proof, uncovered, on the sheet pan or in the loaf pan, in a warm place for 30 minutes before baking.

**Preheat:** While the dough is proofing, preheat the oven to 375°F (190°C).

Scent is a powerful memory-creating sense! Take a few minutes while shaping together and ask your kids what memories they associate with what they are doing. Offer some of your own memories and let them connect the thread of scent and memory to quality time with a favorite adult.

**Brush with Egg Wash:** If desired, beat the egg with a fork in a small bowl and brush each pain au lait with egg wash after proofing. This will give the bread a shiny appearance.

**Bake:** Bake the rolls for 18 to 25 minutes, until golden brown. A loaf will bake in 28 to 30 minutes. Peek halfway through the bake time and rotate the pan for a more even bake. Check the rolls on the early side to ensure they don't overbake.

**Cool:** Let the rolls cool on the sheet pan for about 15 minutes. An adult with oven mitts should unmold the loaf from the pan right away and transfer to a wire rack to let cool for 30 minutes; leaving it in the pan can steam the sides of the loaf, making it too soft and difficult to slice.

Small breads tend to go stale quickly, so they are best when eaten within 2 days. Store them in a resealable plastic bag to keep them soft. For a loaf, slice before storing in a resealable plastic bag for up to 2 days.

>>> turn the page for a fresh jam recipe!

### >>> Raspberry Jam

This is a quick and simple jam that requires nothing more laborious than a bit of stirring. The inclusion of star anise in this recipe was inspired by my friend pastry chef Mary Denham. My kids all think her jam tastes exactly like old-fashioned hard candy, and they especially love it paired with milk bread embedded with chocolate.

*Makes 1½ cups (500 g)*

| INGREDIENT | WEIGHT | VOLUME |
|---|---|---|
| Raspberries | 250 g | 2 cups |
| Finely grated zest and juice of 1 lemon | | |
| Whole star anise (optional) | | 2 |
| Sugar | 210 g | 1 cup |

In a medium saucepan over low heat, combine the raspberries, lemon zest, and lemon juice. Add the star anise, if desired. Stir gently for a few minutes until the berries start to break down.

Add the sugar incrementally, letting it dissolve completely before adding more. When all the sugar has been added, let the jam come to a simmer for about 5 minutes, or until a thermometer reaches 220°F (104°C). Turn off the heat and let the jam cool and set.

 Your young person can stand on a stool and stir the jam carefully with a wooden spoon. Be aware that the jam will be very hot, so gentle, supervised stirring is key!

Remove and discard the star anise and pour the jam into a very clean jar with a lid. It will keep in the fridge for up to a week.

# Sweet Dreams Bunny Bread

In my experience, one of the most challenging parts of having smaller kids is getting them to bed. These soft, chamomile tea–infused rolls are perfect for those nights when bedtime is hardest. Make this dough in the afternoon and you can bake the rolls by bedtime. My kids have grown up loving the magical power of herbal tea, knowing that some flowers like lavender and chamomile can help us have sweet dreams.

Makes 8 to 10 rolls

| INGREDIENT | WEIGHT | VOLUME |
|---|---|---|
| Water | 600 g | 2½ cups |
| Chamomile flowers | 1 g | 2 teaspoons (see Note) |
| Culinary lavender flowers | 2 g | 1 tablespoon |

Note: If you don't have chamomile flowers, use 4 tea bags, preferably Traditional Medicinals chamomile lavender or Celestial Seasonings Sleepytime.

| For the Dough: | | |
|---|---|---|
| Premade tea | 280 g | 1 cup plus 2 tablespoons |
| Honey (or any liquid sweetener you like) | 40 g | 2 tablespoons |
| Canola oil or other neutral oil | 50 g | ¼ cup |
| Instant yeast | 12 g | 1 rounded tablespoon |
| All-purpose flour | 500 g | 4 cups |
| Fine salt | 10 g | 1½ teaspoons |

**Make the Tea:** In a medium saucepan over medium-high heat, bring the water to a simmer. Add the flowers and turn off the heat. Cover and let steep for 4 hours or overnight. Pass through a strainer to remove the botanicals, or simply remove the tea bags before using. Note: Half of the tea mixture will be used to make the dough; the rest can be reserved for drinking. If you are using real flowers, let your little one pluck the flower heads from the stems for some sensory play.

**Prepare:** Use the temperature chart (see page 27) to prepare the tea to the correct temperature. Keep in mind that on cooler days (below 75°F/23°C) the dough may take a bit longer to rise. On warmer days (above 75°F/23°C) the dough may rise more quickly. Weigh or measure all the ingredients and gather your supplies.

**Mix:** To make the dough, in a large bowl, combine about half the tea (280 g) with the honey, oil, and yeast. Use a spoon to mix gently until the yeast is dispersed. Add the flour and salt. Mix by hand, using a grab-and-squish motion to thoroughly combine all the ingredients. Alternatively, use a wooden spoon to mix. The dough is well mixed when it is smooth and there are no dry bits of flour. This may take about 5 minutes.

**Rest:** Cover the bowl with a kitchen towel and set aside to let the dough rest, relax, and rehydrate for 15 minutes.

continued

**Knead:** Turn the dough out onto a lightly floured work surface. Knead the dough with a push-and-fold motion. Firmly push the dough away from you, then fold it back toward you, rotating the dough a quarter turn every few folds. Repeat pushing and folding for about 5 minutes, or until the dough feels smooth, tight, and bouncy.

**Rise:** Return the dough to the bowl, cover it with a kitchen towel (or plastic wrap, if necessary, in drier climates), and let rise for 90 minutes.

**Divide and Shape:** Line a sheet pan with parchment paper. Turn the dough out onto a lightly floured work surface. Divide the dough into 8 to 10 pieces, roughly 75 grams each. To form the dough into rolls, gently roll the dough between both hands with a soft rounding motion, like you'd do with clay. Place the rolls on the prepared sheet pan spaced evenly apart.

**Proof:** Let the rolls proof, uncovered, at room temperature on the sheet pan for 30 minutes before baking.

**Preheat:** While the rolls are proofing, preheat the oven to 375°F (190°C).

If your little ones want to help shape the rolls, have them pretend they're making a sphere from clay—it's the same motion.

**Make Bunnies:** To shape bunnies, gently pinch one end of a roll to make an egg shape; this is the front of your bunny. To form ears, use scissors to snip 2 little ear shapes directly into the sphere and pull up a little piece for each ear. Use a chopstick to poke little dents below to make the eyes. For best results, do this just before baking. Repeat with each roll.

**Bake:** Bake for 18 to 25 minutes, until light golden brown. Peek halfway through the bake time and rotate the pan for a more even bake. Check the rolls on the early side to ensure they don't overbake.

**Cool:** Let the rolls cool on the sheet pan for about 15 minutes.

Small breads tend to go stale quickly, so they are best when eaten within 2 days. Store them in a resealable plastic bag to keep them soft.

 **tea** When you are ready for tea before bed, simply rewarm the rest of the steeped tea, adding milk and honey to taste.

Try letting your child cut the bunny ears. It's okay if they aren't perfect—funny little creatures are fun, too! Using safety scissors at different angles is a great hand skill to practice here.

# Winter Warming Spices Bread

Traditional warming spices infuse this sweet dough, which is based on the flavor profile of gingerbread. Enjoy it alongside a cup of hot cocoa and make paper snowflakes for your window, dehydrated oranges, popcorn garlands, or whatever sweet handicrafts you love in winter. Doing this year after year can become a beautiful family tradition.

*Makes 1 loaf*

| INGREDIENT | WEIGHT | VOLUME |
|---|---|---|
| Water | 270 g | 1 cup plus 2 tablespoons |
| Dark brown sugar | 50 g | ¼ cup unpacked |
| Unsalted butter, melted and cooled | 50 g | 3½ tablespoons |
| Medium egg, beaten | | 1 |
| Instant yeast | 14 g | 1½ tablespoons |
| Molasses | 20 g | 1 tablespoon |
| All-purpose flour | 460 g | 3¾ cups plus 2 tablespoons |
| Ground cinnamon | 6 g | 1 tablespoon |
| Ground ginger | 4 g | 2 teaspoons |
| Ground nutmeg | 2 g | 1 teaspoon |
| Fine salt | 10 g | 1½ teaspoons |
| Finely grated zest of 1 orange | | |
| Egg (optional, for egg wash) | | 1 |

**Prepare:** Use the temperature chart (see page 27) to prepare the water to the correct temperature. Keep in mind that on cooler days (below 75°F/23°C) the dough may take a bit longer to rise. On warmer days (above 75°F/23°C) the dough may rise more quickly. Weigh or measure all the ingredients and gather your supplies.

**Mix:** In a large bowl, combine the water, brown sugar, butter, the first egg, yeast, and molasses. Use a spoon to mix gently until the yeast is dispersed. Add the flour, cinnamon, ginger, nutmeg, salt, and orange zest. Mix by hand, using a grab-and-squish motion to thoroughly combine all the ingredients. Alternatively, use a wooden spoon to mix. The dough is well mixed when it is smooth and there are no dry bits of flour. This may take about 5 minutes.

**Rest:** Cover the bowl with a kitchen towel and set aside to let the dough rest, relax, and rehydrate for 15 minutes.

**Knead:** Turn the dough out onto a lightly floured work surface. Knead the dough with a push-and-fold motion. Firmly push the dough away from you, then fold it back toward you, rotating the dough a quarter turn every few folds. Repeat pushing and folding for about 5 minutes, or until the dough feels smooth, tight, and bouncy.

**Rise:** Return the dough to the bowl, cover it with a kitchen towel (or plastic wrap, if necessary, in drier climates), and let rise for 90 minutes.

**Divide and Shape:** Turn the dough out onto a lightly floured work surface. Divide the dough into 6 pieces, roughly

150 grams each. Gently round the pieces into balls and then nestle them into a 9 by 5-inch (23 by 13 by 6 cm) loaf pan side by side and press them down into the pan. The dough balls will rise together to make a cohesive loaf with a bumpy top.

**Proof:** Let the dough proof, uncovered, at room temperature in the loaf pan for 1½ to 2 hours before baking. A good proof is very important to the texture of this dough and keeping it warm is crucial to achieving a tall, fully proofed loaf. If the loaf is proofing very slowly, place it in a closed, turned-off oven with the light on and set a pan of boiling water on the shelf underneath it. This will provide the gentle, steamy heat needed to proof the dough. A fully proofed loaf should rise above the edges of the pan and leave a soft impression when you press on it.

**Preheat:** After the dough has proofed, preheat the oven to 375°F (190°C). If you were proofing your dough in the unheated oven, be sure to take it out before turning on the oven!

**Brush with Egg Wash:** If desired, beat the second egg with a fork in a small bowl and brush the loaf with egg wash after proofing.

**Bake:** Bake for 25 to 30 minutes, until deep golden brown. Peek halfway through the bake time and rotate the pan for a more even bake. Check the loaf on the early side to ensure it doesn't overbake.

**Cool:** An adult with oven mitts should unmold the loaf from the pan right away and transfer to a wire rack to let cool for 30 minutes; leaving it in the pan can steam the sides of the loaf, making it too soft and difficult to slice.

This bread stays fresh for up to 4 days. Slice the loaf and store it in a resealable plastic bag to keep it soft.

Some children don't mind getting their hands a bit messy, but others might. If they are so inclined, they can help mix the dough by dumping each ingredient into a large bowl.

>>> see page 70 for a delicious drink recipe to sip with this bread!

winter warming spices bread, page 66

>>> **Hot Chocolate with Homemade Whipped Cream**

Dip your Winter Warming Spices Bread into this decadent hot chocolate for the perfect treat after a day of ice skating or other outdoor fun. I prefer dark chocolate for this, but you can use any nice chocolate bar that your family likes.     *Serves 2 or 3 little people*

| INGREDIENT | WEIGHT | VOLUME |
|---|---|---|
| **For the Whipped Cream:** | | |
| Heavy whipping cream | 240 g | 1 cup |
| Sugar | 13 g | 1 tablespoon |
| Pure vanilla extract | 4 g | 1 teaspoon |
| **For the Hot Chocolate:** | | |
| Whole milk (or alternative of choice) | 480 g | 2 cups |
| Chocolate of your choice, finely chopped | 100 g | ⅔ cup |
| Raw sugar (turbinado or Demerara) | 13 g | 1 tablespoon |

**Prepare:** To make the whipped cream, place a large metal bowl, whisk, and the heavy whipping cream in the fridge. Cold utensils will make hand-whipping the cream easier.

You can do this in a kitchen mixer, but with kids it's way more fun to whip by hand.

**Warm:** To make the hot chocolate, in a medium saucepan, heat the milk. For kids' drinks I aim for 130°F (54°C); adults typically prefer their drinks closer to 160°F (71°C). Another tried-and-true method for cooling down kids' drinks is to shield them with extra (cold) whipped cream! Remove the milk from the heat when the desired temperature is reached, then stir in the chocolate and raw sugar until melted and well combined.

**Whip:** Remove the bowl, whisk, and heavy whipping cream from the fridge, pour the cream into the bowl, and whisk vigorously until thickened. Whisk in the sugar and vanilla. When the whipped cream forms a soft peak on the end of the whisk, it's done. Be sure not to overwhip, which will make the cream become chunky in texture.

Scoop dollops of whipped cream into mugs of warm hot chocolate and enjoy with spiced bread.

Kids can help whip the cream by hand, taking turns if there is more than one child, whipping vigorously with the whisk until the cream begins to hold its shape.

# Cookie Bread (Conchas/Melonpan)

Many cultures enjoy an enriched bread with a colored cookie topping baked onto it. Mexican conchas are marked on top to resemble seashells, and Japanese melonpan are crosshatched to look a bit like pineapples. These are surprisingly easy to make, and kids can practice a new skill of making the cookie dough topping.

This recipe is an adaptation from my friend Yukimi Masuda's recipe, which she makes at her bakery, Bread House Nest, in Chiba, Japan.

*Makes 12 rolls*

| INGREDIENT | WEIGHT | VOLUME |
| --- | --- | --- |
| **For the Dough:** | | |
| Whole milk | 150 g | ⅔ cup |
| Medium egg | | 1 |
| Unsalted butter, melted and cooled | 30 g | 2 tablespoons |
| Instant yeast | 8 g | 2½ teaspoons |
| Granulated sugar | 20 g | 1½ teaspoons |
| All-purpose flour | 300 g | 2½ cups |
| Fine salt | 3 g | ½ teaspoon |
| **For the Cookie Dough Topping:** | | |
| Unsalted butter, at room temperature | 70 g | 5 tablespoons |
| Brown sugar | 75 g | ⅓ cup unpacked |
| Medium egg, beaten | | 1 |
| Pure vanilla extract | 3 g | ¾ teaspoon |
| Baking powder | 1 g | ¼ teaspoon |
| All-purpose flour | 185 g | 1½ cups, plus additional if needed |
| **For the Conchas:** | | |
| Food coloring (pink and yellow are the most common) | | 5 drops |

**Prepare:** Use the temperature chart (see page 27) to prepare the milk to the correct temperature. Keep in mind that on cooler days (below 75°F/23°C) the dough may take a bit longer to rise. On warmer days (above 75°F/23°C) the dough may rise more quickly. Weigh or measure all the ingredients and gather your supplies.

**Mix:** To make the dough, in a large bowl, combine the milk, egg, butter, yeast, and granulated sugar. Use a spoon to mix gently until the yeast is dispersed. Add the flour and salt. Mix by hand, using a grab-and-squish motion to thoroughly combine all the ingredients. Alternatively, use a wooden spoon to mix. The dough is well mixed when it is smooth and there are no dry bits of flour. This may take about 5 minutes.

**Rest:** Cover the bowl with a kitchen towel and set aside to let the dough rest, relax, and rehydrate for 15 minutes.

**Knead:** Turn the dough out onto a lightly floured work surface. Knead the dough with a push-and-fold motion. Firmly push the dough away from you, then fold it back toward you, rotating the dough a quarter turn every few folds. Repeat pushing and folding for about 5 minutes, or until the dough feels smooth, tight, and bouncy.

**Rise:** Return the dough to the bowl, cover it with a kitchen towel (or plastic wrap, if necessary, in drier climates), and let rise for 90 minutes.

continued

Let children mold the cookie dough into rounds using the clay-rounding method or by rolling between two hands. Ask them if it feels too sticky—this is good sensory information to judge. If the cookie dough sticks, dust their hands or the cookie ball lightly with flour to make it easier to handle.

**Make the Cookie Dough Topping:** While the dough is rising, in a medium bowl, use a wooden spoon to cream together the butter and brown sugar. Stir in the beaten egg and vanilla slowly, following with the baking powder, then the flour.

If making conchas, use a spoon to mix the food coloring into the cookie topping until it is well combined. If making melonpan, you don't need to add any coloring.

Check the texture of the cookie dough. It should be tacky but firm like cookie dough, so you can shape it into balls. Depending on the type of butter you used, you may need to add a couple tablespoons more flour. If the dough has the texture of frosting, it needs a bit more flour.

Line a sheet pan with parchment paper. Portion the cookie dough into 12 little balls, roughly 30 grams each, then place them on the prepared pan. Cover with plastic wrap, then freeze until the bread dough finishes rising; this will make them easier to work with.

**Divide and Shape:** Line another sheet pan with parchment paper. Turn the bread dough out onto a lightly floured work surface. Divide the dough into 12 pieces, roughly 45 grams each. To shape, round each piece gently into a ball and place on the prepared pan spaced evenly apart.

**Top with Cookie Dough:** Flatten each ball of cookie dough between two sheets of parchment paper until it is a flat circle, then use your hand to form it gently onto the top of each roll. If the cookie dough gets warm, sticky, and difficult to handle, return it to the freezer for 10 minutes.

Start by demonstrating, then let the children follow you, marking the cookie dough with the knife themselves. It's fun to do and good practice for fine motor skills.

**Decorate:**

**For conchas:** Use a small knife to make a series of curved lines over the colored cookie topping to resemble a seashell.

**For melonpan:** Use a small knife to make a crosshatch pattern through the cookie dough.

**Proof:** Let the rolls proof, uncovered, at room temperature on the sheet pan for 30 minutes before baking.

**Preheat:** While the rolls are proofing, preheat the oven to 325°F (170°C).

**Bake:** Bake for 13 to 15 minutes, until the rolls are a very light golden brown underneath. Check them on the early side to ensure they don't overbake.

**Cool:** Let the rolls cool on the sheet pan for about 15 minutes.

Small breads tend to go stale quickly, so they are best when eaten within 2 days. Store them in a resealable plastic bag to keep them soft.

# Springtime Tie-Dye or Rainbow Bread

Springtime evokes a beautiful array of colors and acts as inspiration for this rainbow-laced bread. The bread is a one-third quantity recipe, so you can make the dough three times using three different colors, or you can use as many colors as you like. Just repeat the recipe for each individual color, making each separately. (If you combine them too early, you will just get brown dough when all the colors mix together!) At the end, fold them together to make tie-dye or rainbow bread. This recipe is a little advanced, but it's a great opportunity to make something fun with friends!

*Makes 8 small rolls of tie-dye bread (3 colors) or 2 loaves of rainbow bread (6 colors)*

| INGREDIENT | WEIGHT | VOLUME |
|---|---|---|
| **Per dough (total for rolls/ total for loaves)** | | |
| Water | 100 g (300 g/ 600 g) | ¼ cup plus 2 tablespoons (1 cup/2 cups) |
| Food coloring, 3 to 6 colors | | (5 drops per color) |
| Honey (or any liquid sweetener you like) | 20 g (60g/ 120 g) | 1 tablespoon (3 tablespoons/ 6 tablespoons) |
| Canola oil or other neutral oil | 16 g (48 g/ 96 g) | 1 tablespoon plus 1 teaspoon (4 tablespoons/ 7 tablespoons) |
| Instant yeast | 6 g (18 g/ 36 g) | 2 teaspoons (6 teaspoons/ 12 teaspoons) |
| All-purpose flour | 150 g (450 g/ 900 g) | 1¼ cups (3¾ cups/ 7½ cups) |
| Fine salt | 4 g (12 g/ 24 g) | ½ rounded teaspoon (1½ teaspoons/ 3 teaspoons) |
| Egg (optional, for egg wash) | | 1 (3/6) |

**Prepare:** Use the temperature chart (see page 27) to prepare the water to the correct temperature. Keep in mind that on cooler days (below 75°F/23°C) the dough may take a bit longer to rise. On warmer days (above 75°F/23°C) the dough may rise more quickly. Weigh or measure all the ingredients and gather your supplies. Combine each color of dye that you are using with 100 grams of water. If you are making rolls with 3 colors, you could have 3 bowls of dyed water. If you are making loaves with 6 colors, you could have 6 bowls of dyed water.

**Mix:** In a medium bowl, combine one of the dyed waters, honey, oil, and yeast. Use a spoon to mix gently until the yeast is dispersed. Add the flour and salt. Mix by hand, using a grab-and-squish motion to thoroughly combine all the ingredients. Alternatively, use a wooden spoon to mix. The dough is well mixed when it is smooth and there are no dry bits of flour. This may take about 5 minutes. Repeat with each dye color to make 3 or 6 different-colored doughs.

Food coloring offers a great opportunity to talk about primary colors, complementary colors, favorite colors, springtime colors, and the order of the rainbow.

**Rest:** Set the doughs aside in separate bowls, cover with kitchen towels, and let rest, relax, and hydrate for 15 minutes.

Remember, kids will develop hand skills as they mix, knead, and shape dough. Check in with them at any time and ask them what they can feel, taste, smell, or hear.

**Knead:** Turn each color of the dough out onto a lightly floured work surface. Knead the dough with a push-and-fold motion. Firmly push the dough away from you, then fold it back toward you, rotating the dough a quarter turn every few folds. Repeat pushing and folding for about 5 minutes, or until the dough feels smooth, tight, and bouncy.

**Rise:** Press each dough out into a flat rectangle with your hands. Stack the colors on top of one another (for rainbow bread, start with red on bottom, followed by orange, yellow, green, blue, and purple; for tie-dye rolls, use any color order you like). Transfer the stacked doughs to a large bowl. The colored doughs will rise together in a bit of a randomized pattern, like tie-dye. Cover the bowl with a kitchen towel (or plastic wrap, if necessary, in drier climates), and let rise for 45 minutes. The dough should roughly double in size.

**Shape:** Gently turn the dough out onto a lightly floured work surface, being careful to preserve the color order (or not— either way will be okay).

**To make tie-dye rolls:** Line a sheet pan with parchment paper. Divide the dough into 8 pieces, roughly 200 grams each, making sure to get all the colors in each piece. Use your hands to round the dough into balls; as you do this, the colors will swirl together like tie-dye. Place the rolls on the prepared sheet pan spaced evenly apart.

**To make rainbow loaves:** Divide the dough in half. Set one piece on your work surface. The red should be on the bottom, with all the other colors on top of it. Gently pat the dough out into a rough square shape. Fold in the corners farthest from you to meet in the middle, as if you were folding in the sleeves of a T-shirt, then roll the dough up toward you like a yoga mat. Place it in a 9 by 5-inch (23 by 13 by 6 cm) loaf pan with the seam side down. Repeat with the other piece of dough to make a second loaf.

continued

**Proof:** Let the rolls proof, uncovered, at room temperature on the sheet pan for 30 to 45 minutes, until soft and pillowy. Loaves may take an hour or more to rise. A fully proofed loaf should rise above the edges of the pan and leave a soft impression when you press on it.

**Preheat:** While the rolls or loaves are proofing, preheat the oven to 350°F (180°C).

**Bake:** Bake the rolls for 18 to 20 minutes, or bake the loaves for 25 to 30 minutes, until golden brown. Peek halfway through the bake time and rotate the pan for a more even bake. Check on the early side to ensure the rolls or bread don't overbake.

**Cool:** Let the rolls cool on the sheet pan for about 15 minutes. An adult with oven mitts should unmold each loaf from the pan right away and transfer to a wire rack to let cool for 30 minutes; leaving it in the pan can steam the sides of the loaf, making it too soft and difficult to slice. A slice should reveal a beautiful rainbow!

This bread stays fresh for up to 4 days. To keep the bread soft, store it in a resealable plastic bag. Slice loaves before storing.

## watercolor painting

While the bread is proofing, baking, and cooling, it can be hard to wait for the final result! This is a great time to get out some watercolors and play. Paint rainbows, mix colors, and talk about what you see and how the different colors make you feel. Experiment with brushes or painting with fingers and talk about favorite experiences with color (You sure love that blue shirt! I noticed you picked a yellow flower today!). I always suggest the Dr. Seuss book *My Many Colored Days*, which connects colors to emotions and is great for toddlers through age 9 or so. We can use our hands to create beauty, appreciate the world, and express ourselves and our emotions.

# Seasonal Breads

RECIPES TO CONNECT WITH NATURE,
FOR AGES 7 TO 10

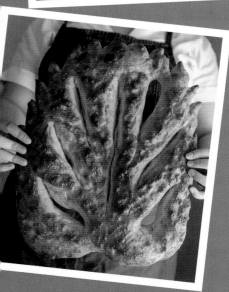

# In This Chapter

## You will practice . . .

* Folding lean doughs
* Incorporating seasonal ingredients into breads
* Dimpling focaccia and stretching pizza

Food is the perfect avenue for exploring the seasons and how they shape your local foodshed, whether in your own garden or at the local farmers' market. Recipes in this chapter focus on engaging with your environment and introduce concepts of community, seasonality, and locality.

These seasonal breads are made with what I call Adventure Dough, a simple, lean dough composed of just flour, yeast, salt, and water. This lean dough can be used to make all sorts of great crunchy breads: a loaf perfect for a picnic (page 89), crunchy seedy twisty breadsticks for dipping (page 99), a beautiful focaccia (page 94), a summer garden pizza (page 113), thin crispy crackers (page 127), and so much more.

The chapter is arranged by season and intended to allow you to bake with local produce throughout the year. Many of the fresh ingredients might even be in your home garden—or inspire you to start one if you haven't already. Accompanying recipes for dressings and dips further encourage seasonal eating. The payoff to all this learning, practicing, and growing is a lifetime of eating well and loving the earth.

# Learning Opportunities

Use bread baking to encourage your child's curiosity about the world around them, their greater community, and how it all fits together. Kids this age begin to seek adventure, take healthy risks, and try new things. Baking seasonal breads will be a gateway to exploring the following concepts.

## Weather Observation

Bread baking can help kids understand weather and temperature. Open the weather app on your phone to do a temperature check at the beginning of baking time, and have a chat about how hot or cold it is outside, how the temperature will affect your bake, and how the weather changes with the seasons.

## Journaling/Note Taking

Keep a baking journal (see page 86). The practice of making notes and observations about processes and environments is a great habit to start and will serve kids well in their studies or hobbies outside the kitchen. Noticing, describing, and even sketching the world around us is a wonderful practice for a lifelong learning adventure.

## Weights and Measures

Comparing weights and measures is a key concept in baking. Your child can likely weigh the ingredients on the scale themselves, perhaps with a little help. You can help them notice the differences in the weights and volumes of ingredients.

## Connecting with Nature

Planting a small garden or an herb pot with your children or visiting your local farmers' market is a lovely way to get little ones acquainted with the seasonality of food. They'll begin to understand when snap peas may bloom, when radishes grow, and when strawberries start to taste the sweetest. Growing a beautiful tomato from a seed in your own garden is the kind of small but profound experience worth the time investment.

# Keeping a Baker's Notebook

Each time you bake bread is like running an experiment. Keeping a notebook will help you start to notice more details about the baking process, and over time, patterns will emerge. Have your child pick out a baking notebook, decorate it with stickers or drawings, and begin to take notes about the breads. Think about your own goals and desires in the details of your bread. If you are very satisfied, how will you replicate your success? If you see room for improvement, what would you adjust next time? Baking skill has a way of developing in cycles: It seems that as soon as you feel a bit overconfident, you'll have a tough bake that turns out less than perfect. What changed? When you go back to your notes, you will usually realize the solutions are already there. This deeper understanding will allow you to eventually test out new ideas and someday create your own recipes.

## What to Look For

Evaluating your bread is an important part of the process, but try not to be overly critical of your work or to cancel out the joy of creating something homemade and delicious. Remember that you can use what you learn from this go-round to tweak your process the next time. Here are some things you can think about, observe, and note in your journal:

**1**

### AESTHETICS

How does the bread look? Is it even and beautifully browned, or is it pale in some places and overbaked in others? Is the shape uniform and rounded, or is it lumpy and misshapen? Misshapen bread can be corrected with a little more patience and diligence as you shape the dough. A pale or an unevenly browned loaf can be the result of over-proofing or an error in oven temperature.

## CRUST

Is the crust thin and crispy or thick and chewy? A thin, crisp crust is usually the result of a lower-hydration dough baked at a higher heat for a shorter amount of time. A thicker crust may develop when there is more water in the dough, more steam in the oven, or a slightly lower baking temperature with a longer baking time. Think about your goals and adjust accordingly.

## CRUMB

The interior, or crumb, depends on a few factors, the first being the type of bread. Enriched breads should have a fine, uniform cakelike crumb. Lean doughs will have a more irregular and open crumb structure. The interior of the bread is affected by the quality of mixing, rising, and proofing. If the crumb has large gaping holes, this may be the result of a shaping error, where large pockets of air have been trapped inside the dough during shaping.

## FLAVOR

When tasting your bread, try closing your eyes and focusing on what flavors come to you. Some words to help you identify the flavors are earthy (think mushrooms), tangy (yogurt), nutty (almonds), and sweet (honey). Does the crust have a sweetness from caramelization? Is the crumb tangy or sweet, or does it taste clean, like wheat? Fermentation is one of the key factors in final flavor. An overly tangy or sour loaf may have had longer fermentation than was necessary or risen at a too warm temperature.

Here are some variables I recommend tracking. Consider making these headings in your notebook to log notes about every bake.

Recipe/Ambient Temperature/Final Dough Temperature/Bulk Rise Time/Proofing Time/Baking Temperature and Time/Results/Ideas for Next Time

# Anytime Adventure Bread

You'll want to tackle this recipe before making the others in this chapter. This recipe is a typical dough that bakers call a "straight lean dough," which means it isn't usually enriched with any butter, sweeteners, or eggs and is relatively straightforward to make. Many bread products are lean doughs like this, including sandwich loaves, pizza, baguettes, and breadsticks. Practice making this dough in a simple loaf pan and then move on to try new shapes, baking methods, and seasonal toppings in the following recipes.     *Makes 1 loaf*

| INGREDIENT | WEIGHT | VOLUME |
|---|---|---|
| Water | 280 g | 1 cup plus 2½ tablespoons |
| Instant yeast | 7 g | 2¼ teaspoons |
| All-purpose flour | 300 g | 2½ cups |
| Whole wheat flour | 100 g | ¾ cup plus 2 tablespoons |
| Fine salt | 8 g | 1 rounded teaspoon |

Kids ages 7 and older should be able to mix this dough themselves and will likely delight in the opportunity to do so.

**Prepare:** Use the temperature chart (see page 27) to prepare the water to the correct temperature. Keep in mind that on cooler days (below 75°F/23°C) the dough may take a bit longer to rise. On warmer days (above 75°F/23°C) the dough may rise more quickly. Weigh or measure all the ingredients and gather your supplies.

**Mix:** Begin by pouring the water into a large bowl. Add the yeast and dissolve it into the water by swishing it around with your hands. Add both flours and the salt. Mix by hand, using a grab-and-squish motion to combine. You may need to hold the bowl for your kids so they can actively mix with both hands. If your child is resistant to having messy hands, use a wooden spoon to combine the ingredients. As the shaggy soft dough comes together, it will be a little bit sticky and tacky; this is okay. Your main goal is to fully combine all the ingredients. Make sure there are no clumps of flour or dry spots and aim for a smooth dough at the finish.

**Rest:** Let the dough rest in the bowl, uncovered, at room temperature for 30 minutes.

**Fold:** You will bring this dough together with a folding motion, moving your hands around the bowl and stretching the dough as you do so, then pulling it toward you. This is the same idea as kneading but you are leaving this slightly wetter dough in the bowl and performing the action by stretching the dough away and then folding it back to you.

continued

## anytime adventure bread, continued

Watching the dough come together may seem like magic! As the gluten develops, the dough becomes stronger—which is just as good as magic when it comes to baking bread. Ask your kid what changes they can see in the dough as you work through the folds together. They may notice that the dough becomes less stretchy and much stronger with each fold!

Explain to your kids that shaping the dough is like folding a shirt. You fold in the sides like you fold in the sleeves.

Work like this around the bowl until the dough seems to form a tight ball.

**Rise:** Cover the bowl with a kitchen towel (or plastic wrap, if necessary, in drier climates), and let rise for 90 minutes.

**Shape:** Scrape the dough gently out of the bowl (all in one piece, without tearing it) onto a moderately floured work surface. Gently pat the dough out into a rough square shape. Fold in the sides of the dough a bit to create a rectangle shape, then roll the dough up toward you like a yoga mat. Place it in a 9 by 5-inch (23 by 13 by 6 cm) loaf pan with the seam side down. Whatever shape it ends up being is fine and part of the learning process. If it seems very crooked, gently press the dough down into the pan so it takes the shape of the rectangular pan.

**Proof:** Let the loaf proof, uncovered, at room temperature in the pan for 45 minutes to an hour. A fully proofed loaf should rise above the edges of the pan and leave a soft impression when you press on it.

**Preheat:** While the loaf is proofing, preheat the oven to 425°F (220°C).

**Bake:** Bake for 35 to 40 minutes, until the loaf is a deep brown color—like a russet potato. (Hopefully the loaf isn't shaped like a potato, but if that happens, that is okay too!) Peek halfway through the bake time and rotate the pan for a more even bake.

**Cool:** An adult with oven mitts should unmold the loaf from the pan right away and transfer to a wire rack to let cool for 30 minutes; leaving it in the pan can steam the sides of the loaf, making it too soft and difficult to slice.

This bread stays fresh for 3 to 4 days. Store in a beeswax wrap at room temperature.

# Butter and Radish Toasts

Growing radishes is surprisingly easy, and they grow quite quickly so you can eat radishes all spring! We like growing French breakfast radishes because they are a lovely pink color and not quite as spicy as other radishes. Butter and radish toasts are refreshing to eat for an afternoon snack with a cup of tea.

Makes 2

| INGREDIENT | WEIGHT | VOLUME |
|---|---|---|
| 2 slices Anytime Adventure Bread (page 89) | | |
| Unsalted butter, at room temperature | 60 g | 4 tablespoons |
| Pinch of flaky sea salt | | |
| French breakfast radishes, thinly sliced | | 2 |

Toast the bread slices to your liking—or, if you prefer, skip the toasting and enjoy the soft bread. Thickly butter the toast and sprinkle with flaky salt.

Arrange the thin radish rounds all over the buttery toasts before eating.

# All-Year Herb Croutons

If you don't finish a loaf of bread before it goes stale, it doesn't have to go to waste; you can repurpose it into croutons. Though springtime is a wonderful time for fresh herbs, you can make these year-round with dried herbs, too. Learning not to waste resources is a valuable skill to hold on to. Reduce, reuse, recycle!

*Makes about 2 cups (500 g), depending on how much stale bread you have*

| INGREDIENT | WEIGHT | VOLUME |
| --- | --- | --- |
| The stale remains of a loaf of bread | | |
| Garlic (optional) | | 1 clove |
| Olive oil | 50 to 60 g | ¼ to ⅓ cup, as needed |
| Fresh herbs, such as rosemary, oregano, chives, and thyme, finely chopped | 3 to 6 g | 1 to 2 tablespoons |
| Pinch of salt | | |
| Coarsely ground black pepper | | |
| Grated Parmesan cheese (optional) | | |

Preheat the oven to 400°F (200°C).

Tear the bread by hand over a large bowl into evenly sized pieces; you can use any size you like so long as they are easy to chew. Or, if you prefer, use a knife to cut the bread into cubes. Similar-size pieces will bake more evenly and help to avoid burning.

If you want to add garlic, use a mortar and pestle to crush it into a paste, then mix it into the oil with a fork. Incorporate the chopped herbs into the oil the same way. Drizzle the olive oil mixture over the bread while tossing with a spoon; start with ¼ cup (50 g) and add a little more if the bread pieces seem dry. Toss to combine. Season with salt and pepper to taste. You can get creative and add a little bit of cheese, too. (Parmesan is a great choice.)

Spread the croutons out in a single layer on a half-sheet pan. Make sure there is space between the croutons so they get crispy all around!

 Little ones can tear the bread, chop the herbs, and season the croutons themselves.

Bake for 12 to 15 minutes, until golden brown. Check the croutons on the early side to ensure they don't burn.

Let cool on the sheet pan for about 10 minutes. You can wait until they are room temperature, but slightly warm croutons are a real treat. Because the bread is already stale and the croutons are crunchy, these are best when eaten the same day!

# Spring/Summer Focaccia

Focaccia is a fun and simple bread to make and a perfect opportunity for self-expression. Have your kids treat focaccia like a blank canvas to decorate any way they'd like. Spring onions can become flower stems, yellow bell peppers can be sunflower petals, onion curls can become crescent moons, little peas can be stars—the opportunities for creativity are endless. If you want a bigger/thicker focaccia, you can double every ingredient in the dough recipe and proceed in the same way; it will fill an entire half-sheet pan.

*Makes 1 focaccia*

| INGREDIENT | WEIGHT | VOLUME |
|---|---|---|
| **For the Toppings:** | | |
| Spring onions, trimmed | | 3 or 4 |
| Yellow bell pepper, cored and trimmed | | 1 |
| Red bell pepper, cored and trimmed | | 1 |
| Handful of cherry tomatoes, cut in half | | |
| Pinch of flaky sea salt (optional) | | |
| **For the Focaccia:** | | |
| Water | 280 g | 1 cup plus 2½ tablespoons |
| Instant yeast | 7 g | 2¼ teaspoons |
| All-purpose flour | 300 g | 2½ cups |
| Whole wheat flour | 100 g | ¾ cup plus 2 tablespoons |
| Fine salt | 8 g | 1 rounded teaspoon |
| Olive oil, for the pan | 25 g | 2 tablespoons |

**Prepare:** Use the temperature chart (see page 27) to prepare the water to the correct temperature. Keep in mind that on cooler days (below 75°F/23°C) the dough may take a bit longer to rise. On warmer days (above 75°F/23°C) the dough may rise more quickly. Weigh or measure all the ingredients and gather your supplies.

Cut the toppings into your desired shapes and sizes for decorating.

**Mix:** To make the focaccia, in a large bowl, combine the water and yeast by swishing it around with your fingers until well dissolved. Add both flours and the salt. Mix by hand, using a grab-and-squish motion to thoroughly combine all the ingredients. Alternatively, use a wooden spoon to mix. The dough is well mixed when it is smooth and there are no dry bits of flour. This may take about 5 minutes.

**Fold:** Bring the dough together with folds. Starting on the side of the bowl closest to you, scoop both hands under the sides of the dough and glide your hands around the perimeter of the bowl, each hand moving on one side in a semicircular motion, gently stretching the dough away from you as you go. Once your hands meet again at the top of the bowl, pull the dough over itself, across the bowl, back toward you. Work like this around the bowl until the dough forms a tight ball.

**Rise:** Cover the bowl with a kitchen towel (or plastic wrap, if necessary, in drier climates), and let rise for 45 minutes.

To even out the focaccia, let kids dimple it gently, using their fingertips to softly "tiptoe" all over the puffy dough. The key here is to be gentle: If you press all the air out of the dough, it will have the texture of a hard cracker after you bake it.

**Shape:** Kids will love to shape and decorate this focaccia. Drizzle a half-sheet pan with an even coating of olive oil to prevent the dough from sticking. Scrape the dough out of the bowl onto the prepared sheet pan in one large piece. Gently stretch the dough into a rectangle not quite as large as the pan. Stretch by gently picking up the dough, holding it over your fists, and letting gravity gently stretch the dough. If the dough feels like it cannot stretch further, let it rest on the counter for 10 minutes, covered with a kitchen towel, before trying again. When you have a flat, roughly 8 by 11-inch (20 by 27 cm) rectangle, it's time to get creative! Create a beautiful scene on your focaccia with spring onions, bell peppers, and cherry tomatoes. Press each vegetable into the dough so it doesn't pop out of the bread when it's baking in the oven.

**Proof:** Let the decorated focaccia proof, uncovered, at room temperature on the sheet pan for about 30 minutes.

**Preheat:** While the focaccia is proofing, preheat the oven to 425°F (220°C). Just before baking, sprinkle the focaccia with flaky sea salt, if desired.

**Bake:** Bake for 25 to 30 minutes, until the focaccia has a deep golden-brown crust. Check the focaccia halfway through the bake time and rotate the pan for a more even bake.

**Cool:** Let the focaccia cool on the pan for 20 to 30 minutes before slicing to maintain the fluffy crumb structure, then cut into squares and enjoy!

The large surface area of this bread makes it go stale quickly, so it's best when eaten within 2 days. Store in a resealable plastic bag.

spring/summer focaccia, page 94

## learning about flowers

The picture book *What's Inside a Flower?*, by Rachel Ignotofsky, is a great read to accompany Spring/Summer Focaccia (page 94), helping you to start a conversation about parts of flowers and how they grow. Many vegetables and fruits come from plants that produce flowers before they become food, or they shoot up flowers after they have grown. Ask kids to take some time to look for fruit and vegetable flowers in your community. Do you spy cherry and apple blossoms? Tomato flowers? A zucchini blossom at the farmers' market? Getting your little ones curious about where their food comes from and how it grows will make their baking projects all the more exciting.

# Spring Wildflower Seed Twists

In spring the world is covered with poppies and sunflowers. Each year, they drop their seeds in the fall, and the following year they come back multiplied after the spring rains. These breadsticks are a nod to those tasty seeds that grow beautiful spring flowers. Once you've got this method down for making breadsticks, you can flavor them with anything you like; Parmesan cheese with pesto (page 115) is a great choice.

*Makes 4 to 6 breadsticks*

| INGREDIENT | WEIGHT | VOLUME |
|---|---|---|
| Water | 275 g | 1 cup plus 2 tablespoons |
| Instant yeast | 7 g | 2¼ teaspoons |
| All-purpose flour | 300 g | 2½ cups |
| Whole wheat flour | 100 g | ¾ cup plus 2 tablespoons |
| Fine salt | 8 g | 1 rounded teaspoon |
| Olive oil, for brushing | | |
| Sunflower seeds | | |
| Poppy seeds | | |

**Prepare:** Use the temperature chart (see page 27) to prepare the water to the correct temperature. Keep in mind that on cooler days (below 75°F/23°C) the dough may take a bit longer to rise. On warmer days (above 75°F/23°C) the dough may rise more quickly. Weigh or measure all the ingredients and gather your supplies.

**Mix:** In a large bowl, combine the water and yeast by swishing it around with your fingers until well dissolved. Add both flours and the salt. Mix by hand, using a grab-and-squish motion to thoroughly combine all the ingredients. Alternatively, use a wooden spoon to mix. The dough is well mixed when it is smooth and there are no dry bits of flour. This may take about 5 minutes.

**Fold:** Bring the dough together with folds. Starting on the side of the bowl closest to you, scoop both hands under the sides of the dough and glide your hands around the perimeter of the bowl, each hand moving on one side in a semicircular motion, gently stretching the dough away from you as you go. Once your hands meet again at the top of the bowl, pull the dough over itself, across the bowl, back toward you. Work like this around the bowl until the dough forms a tight ball.

**Rise:** Cover the bowl with a kitchen towel (or plastic wrap, if necessary, in drier climates), and let rise for 45 minutes.

continued

**spring wildflower seed twists, continued**

Kids will have fun creating these dough twists. Take each end of the long strips of dough and twist them in opposite directions.

**learning about seeds**

A great companion activity for this recipe would be planting sunflowers and poppies in your own garden, as well as reading *The Tiny Seed* by Eric Carle, about a tiny seed's journey to become a great big flower. We read it at our bakery story time every spring and all the kids love it. Visiting your local nursery and bookstore are wonderful ways to be part of your community in any season! Eating seeds and planting seeds—it all goes together.

**Shape:** Line a sheet pan with parchment paper. Turn the dough out onto a lightly floured work surface. Press (or roll with a rolling pin) the dough into a large, rough rectangle shape about the same size as your sheet pan. Brush the dough with oil and sprinkle with seeds. Fold the dough like a letter to enclose the seeds inside, then press and roll the dough again to about the size of your sheet pan.

To make the breadsticks, use a pizza cutter to cut long strips of dough lengthwise, about 2 inches (5 cm) wide. Twist the pieces of dough to expose the seeds and place the breadsticks on the prepared sheet pan.

**Rest:** Let the breadsticks rest, uncovered, at room temperature on the sheet pan for 30 minutes before baking.

**Preheat:** While the breadsticks are resting, preheat the oven to 425°F (220°C).

**Bake:** Bake for 15 to 18 minutes, until the breadsticks are golden brown. Peek halfway through the bake time and rotate the pan for a more even bake.

**Cool:** Let the breadsticks cool on the sheet pan for about 15 minutes.

They are best when eaten within a few days, while they are still crunchy. Store them in a resealable plastic bag.

**Variations:** Other seasonal ideas for these include filling them with pesto in summer (page 115), roasted garlic in fall (page 126), or a paste of crushed olives, lemon zest, and rosemary or thyme in winter. Just follow the same instructions and swap out the fillings. Be creative and play with the flavors.

# Spring Pressed Flower and Herb Crackers

Pressing flowers is a fun afternoon activity for kids (see page 105). Some widely available edible flowers are pansies, violets, and nasturtiums. Rose petals and sunflower petals are also easy to find and a fun choice. To make sure your flowers are edible, grow them yourself at home or buy them from a local farm, but never pick flowers that may have been sprayed with pesticides. The best part of this recipe is that once you've gone through it a couple of times together, most kids can make the crackers on their own—and children who can entertain themselves by making their own snacks is a powerful thing for any parent! **Makes about 50 crackers, depending on the size of your crackers**

| INGREDIENT | WEIGHT | VOLUME |
|---|---|---|
| **For the Dough:** | | |
| All-purpose flour | 200 g | 1⅔ cups |
| Whole wheat flour | 100 g | ¾ cup plus 2 tablespoons |
| Water | 120 g | ½ cup, plus more as needed |
| Olive oil or any neutral oil | 30 g | ¼ cup plus 2 tablespoons, plus more as needed |
| Sugar | 16 g | 1 rounded tablespoon |
| Fine salt | 5 g | 1 scant teaspoon |
| **For Decorating and Topping:** | | |
| Handful of pressed edible flowers and leafy herbs | | |
| Flaky sea salt | | |

**Prepare:** A day before you are planning to make the crackers, pick your edible flowers and herbs. Place them between 2 sheets of parchment paper under a large, heavy book (such as a textbook) to press them.

When you're ready to bake, weigh or measure all the ingredients and gather your supplies.

**Mix:** To make the dough, in a large bowl, combine both flours with the water, oil, sugar, and salt and mix by hand until you have a smooth dough. This dough will be much stiffer than most bread dough. It should be firm and not sticky, but not too dry either. If there is dry flour left in your bowl, add more oil, 1 teaspoon at a time, until the dough comes together.

**Knead:** Turn the dough out onto a lightly floured work surface. If the dough feels sticky or tacky, dust with small amounts of flour to adjust the consistency while kneading. Knead the dough with a push-and-fold motion. Firmly push the dough away from you, then fold it back toward you, rotating the dough a quarter turn every few folds. Repeat pushing and folding for about 5 minutes, or until the dough feels smooth, tight, and bouncy.

continued

**Rest:** This dough doesn't need to rise at all, but it does need a rest to make it easier to roll out. Wrap it in plastic wrap or beeswax wrap. If you want to make crackers as soon as possible, you can let the dough rest for 30 minutes at room temperature. If you want to make the crackers later, you can rest the dough in the fridge for up to 4 days.

**Preheat:** Preheat the oven to 375°F (190°C).

**Roll:** On a lightly floured work surface, divide the dough in half. Use a lightly floured rolling pin to roll each piece as thin as possible into a large square (roughly 10 by 10 inches/25 by 25 cm). You should have 2 thin (almost translucent) sheets that should be close to the same shape, but perfectionism is not necessary here. Arrange the pressed flowers and herbs on 1 sheet of dough.

Brush the undecorated sheet of dough lightly with oil and place it on top of the decorated sheet, gently pressing the two sheets together to enclose the botanicals. Make sure the dough isn't sticking to the work surface by lifting it up and dusting a bit of flour underneath for good measure. Gently roll the dough a bit further to press the dough sheets together and roll in all directions to release any bubbles caught inside the dough; be careful not to tear apart the flowers and herbs.

Let kids be creative with how they arrange the flower petals and herbs and let them get lost in the moment using their imaginations. They may make a small scene, orient all the petals in a similar direction, or try to space them all evenly.

**Shape:** Line 2 sheet pans with parchment paper. Use cookie cutters to cut the crackers into fun shapes or a pizza cutter to cut them into squares or diamonds. A fluted ravioli/pasta cutter and a ruler can help you cut diamond shapes, giving the crackers a professional, boxed cracker appearance. Place the shaped crackers on the prepared pans. The crackers don't expand at all, so you can put them really close together.

**Finish:** Brush the crackers with oil and sprinkle with flaky sea salt.

**Bake:** The crackers bake quickly. Bake for 14 to 18 minutes, until the crackers are medium golden brown. Peek halfway through the bake time and switch the placement of the sheet pans and rotate them for a more even bake.

**Cool:** Transfer the crackers to a wire rack to keep them crispy. They will cool quickly, in about 10 minutes. Enjoy!

The crackers will keep in an airtight container for about a week.

### pressed flowers

Making pressed flowers is a low-cost activity that you can do with things you find around your home. All you need is a sheet of parchment paper and a few heavy books!

Take a walk around your neighborhood and pick any flowers you find interesting. Bring the flowers home and arrange between 2 pieces of parchment paper; place them in a heavy book to press (I use a huge pastry textbook). In a few days, you'll have beautifully preserved pressed flowers! We often take our flowers and arrange them into a scene, Mod Podge them onto a nice piece of watercolor paper, and frame the results.

Now I have the habit of picking flowers when we go on a trip and closing them in my notebook. Later when I'm home I'll note the date and place of the trip and preserve that moment. You can use this to commemorate all kinds of special days in a simple and sweet way.

>>> see page 107 for a colorful dip for crackers!

# >>> Beet and White Bean Dip

Adding cooked beets to white beans makes for a hot-pink dip that looks stunning on a picnic table display and tastes so good it will be gone in a snap. If you don't have a garden teeming with beets, you can absolutely use canned beets or the precooked and peeled beets often found in the packaged salad section of grocery stores. Canned white beans are just fine, too.

**Makes 2 to 3 cups (600 g)**

| INGREDIENT | WEIGHT | VOLUME |
|---|---|---|
| Cooked beets | 300 g | 1¾ cups |
| White cannellini beans, cooked and drained | 150 g | ¾ cup |
| Tahini or sunflower butter | 100 g | ⅓ cup |
| Fine salt | 12 g | 2 teaspoons |
| Garlic | | 2 cloves |
| Juice of 1 lemon | | |
| Honey (or any liquid sweetener you like) | 42 g | 2 tablespoons |

In a blender or a food processor, combine the beets, beans, tahini, salt, garlic, lemon juice, and honey and puree until smooth. Enjoy with seed twists or crackers. The dip also looks pretty on a cheeseboard next to some beautiful bread.

Store the dip in an airtight container in the fridge for about a week.

# Summer Ficelles with Cherry Tomatoes

*Ficelle* is a French word that means "string" and is a name for a skinny stick of bread. These ficelles are not as refined in shape as a baguette, but they are easy to make and can be used for sandwiches. Tomatoes can be a bit polarizing for kids, but cooked tomatoes in the form of ketchup or sauce on pasta and pizza is almost always a go. In this case, I bet your little ones will eat tomatoes when they're roasted into the crevices of a crusty bread. Make the most of sweet tomato season by tasting, comparing, baking, and finding your favorite varieties together.

*Makes about 4 ficelles*

| INGREDIENT | WEIGHT | VOLUME |
|---|---|---|
| **For the Dough:** | | |
| Water | 275 g | 1 cup plus 2 tablespoons |
| Instant yeast | 7 g | 2¼ teaspoons |
| All-purpose flour | 300 g | 2½ cups |
| Whole wheat flour | 100 g | ¾ cup plus 2 tablespoons |
| Fine salt | 8 g | 1 rounded teaspoon |
| **For the Topping:** | | |
| Cherry tomatoes, halved | 75 g | 1 cup |
| Olive oil | 25 g | 2 tablespoons |
| Salt | 6 g | 1 teaspoon |
| Handful of fresh or dried herbs, such as basil, oregano, thyme, and rosemary, chopped (optional) | | |

**Prepare:** Use the temperature chart (see page 27) to prepare the water to the correct temperature. Keep in mind that on cooler days (below 75°F/23°C) the dough may take a bit longer to rise. On warmer days (above 75°F/23°C) the dough may rise more quickly. Weigh or measure all the ingredients and gather your supplies.

**Mix:** To make the dough, in a large bowl, combine the water and yeast by swishing it around with your fingers until well dissolved. Add both flours and the salt. Mix by hand, using a grab-and-squish motion to thoroughly combine all the ingredients. Alternatively, use a wooden spoon to mix. The dough is well mixed when it is smooth and there are no dry bits of flour. This may take about 5 minutes.

**Fold:** Bring the dough together with folds. Starting on the side of the bowl closest to you, scoop both hands under the sides of the dough and glide your hands around the perimeter of the bowl, each hand moving on one side in a semicircular motion, gently stretching the dough away from you as you go. Once your hands meet again at the top of the bowl, pull the dough over itself, across the bowl, back toward you. Work like this around the bowl until the dough forms a tight ball.

**Rise:** Cover the bowl with a kitchen towel (or plastic wrap, if necessary, in drier climates), and let rise for 45 minutes.

*continued*

Find a magical rainbow of different-colored cherry tomatoes, from purple to red to yellow, at your local farmers' market, or bring home a Sungold plant and have a go at growing tomatoes yourself.

**Prepare the Topping:** In a medium bowl, combine the tomatoes, olive oil, salt, and herbs, if desired. Use a spoon to toss until the tomatoes are fully and evenly coated.

**Shape:** Line a half-sheet pan with parchment paper. Turn the dough out onto a lightly floured work surface and gently stretch into a large rectangle nearly the size of your pan, keeping the dough at an even thickness. Use a pizza cutter to cut the dough into 4 or 5 long, equally thick sticks. Gently place them on the prepared pan, lightly stretching them into long baguette-like sticks. Press the tomato halves into the top of the ficelles, working down the length of the bread. Be sure to press them firmly into the dough so they don't pop out when baking. If you have leftover herb oil in the tomato bowl, you can brush it over the tops of the ficelles.

**Rest:** Let the ficelles rest, uncovered, at room temperature on the pan for 20 minutes.

**Preheat:** While the ficelles are resting, preheat the oven to 425°F (220°C).

**Bake:** Bake for 18 to 24 minutes, rotating the pan halfway through for an even bake, until the bread is golden brown and the tomatoes are roasted.

**Cool:** Let the ficelles cool on the sheet pan for about 15 minutes. Eat them the same day you bake them.

**sandwiches** If you want to use the ficelles for sandwiches, cut them lengthwise. To make BLTs, lay some bacon on a parchment-lined sheet pan and pop it in the oven for 15 minutes while the ficelles are baking. Top the bread with the cooked bacon, some crisp lettuce, and a smear of Homemade Mayo (recipe follows). These crusty breadstick sandwiches hold up great wrapped in wax paper on a hike and look a lot more sophisticated than your average packed sandwich.

# Homemade Mayo

Mayonnaise is a surprisingly simple concoction. It takes about 3 minutes tops to make, and all that whisking is a great way to channel a child's extra energy.

Makes about 1 cup (250 g)

| INGREDIENT | WEIGHT | VOLUME |
|---|---|---|
| Egg yolk | | 1 |
| Pinch of salt | | |
| Olive oil or any neutral oil | 200 g | 1 cup |
| Juice of ½ lemon (optional) | | |

In a large, heavy bowl, whisk the egg yolk and salt. Stream the oil slowly from a cup with a spout while whisking vigorously. The mixture will begin to thicken and turn opaque. Keep whisking and pouring until all the oil is added. Once all the oil is incorporated and the mayo has thickened, whisk in the lemon juice, if desired, and taste. Add a tiny bit more salt or lemon juice as needed.

Hold the bowl while your child does the whisking—or take turns.

Store in the fridge in an airtight container for up to a week.

# Summer Pizza with Mozzarella, Tomato, and Pesto

Nothing delights kids more than making their own pizzas. Once you get used to devoting 5 minutes to mixing up some dough on a Friday afternoon, and you get over the initial learning curve of stretching dough and using a hot oven, you'll see that homemade pizza can actually come together very quickly—and it's certainly more fun than delivery pizza. This recipe makes 4 personal pizzas about the size of a large dinner plate (depending on your stretching skills). You can halve or double this recipe as needed for your family size.

*Makes 4 pizzas*

| INGREDIENT | WEIGHT | VOLUME |
|---|---|---|
| **For the Dough:** | | |
| Water | 700 g | 1¾ cups plus 3 tablespoons |
| Instant yeast | 14 g | 1½ tablespoons |
| All-purpose flour | 750 g | 6¼ cups |
| Whole wheat flour | 250 g | 2 cups plus 2 tablespoons |
| Fine salt | 12 g | 2 teaspoons |
| **For the Toppings:** | | |
| Olive oil (optional) | | |
| Crushed tomatoes | 411 g | 14.5-ounce can |
| Low-moisture mozzarella cheese, torn | 500 g | 2 cups |
| Handful of fresh basil, torn | | |
| Mortar and Pestle Pesto (recipe follows) | | |

**Prepare:** Use the temperature chart (see page 27) to prepare the water to the correct temperature. Keep in mind that on cooler days (below 75°F/23°C) the dough may take a bit longer to rise. On warmer days (above 75°F/23°C) the dough may rise more quickly. Weigh or measure all the ingredients and gather your supplies.

**Mix:** To make the dough, in a large bowl, combine the water and yeast by swishing it around with your fingers until well dissolved. Add both flours and the salt. Mix by hand, using a grab-and-squish motion to thoroughly combine all the ingredients. Alternatively, use a wooden spoon to mix. The dough is well mixed when it is smooth and there are no dry bits of flour. This may take about 5 minutes.

**Fold:** Bring the dough together with folds. Starting on the side of the bowl closest to you, scoop both hands under the sides of the dough and glide your hands around the perimeter of the bowl, each hand moving on one side in a semicircular motion, gently stretching the dough away from you as you go. Once your hands meet again at the top of the bowl, pull the dough over itself, across the bowl, back toward you. Work like this around the bowl until the dough forms a tight ball.

**Rise:** Cover the bowl with a kitchen towel (or plastic wrap, if necessary, in drier climates), and let rise for 45 minutes.

*continued*

**Preheat:** Preheat the oven to 500°F (260°C) (or as hot as your oven will go). If you have a pizza stone, you can preheat that along with the oven. If you don't have one, you can preheat a baking sheet; just turn it upside-down so the rim doesn't get in the way when you slide the pizza onto it.

**Divide and Shape:** Turn the dough out onto a lightly floured work surface. Divide the dough into 4 pieces, roughly 425 grams each, and use your hands to gently form each into a ball.

**Rest:** Dust the dough rounds lightly with flour, cover with a kitchen towel, and let sit at room temperature for at least 15 minutes.

Kids can do a great job of pushing out the dough into a circle! Watch to make sure that they are gentle with the dough so they don't make the middle too thin or tear a hole in the dough. It's best that an adult handles the dough when lifting it from the work surface.

**Shape the Pizzas:** If the dough feels tacky, dust your work surface lightly with flour to prevent sticking or tearing. To shape the pizzas, start by gently pressing down with your fingertips in a circle around the edges of each round; this will create a rim to make the crust. Stretch the dough by picking it up with your knuckles under the rim and letting gravity stretch the dough. Gently rotate the dough across your knuckles, letting the dough stretch in all directions, creating an even circle. Be careful not to poke your fingers through the dough as it gets thinner. When you finish shaping each round of dough, place it on a sheet of parchment paper.

Kids love decorating their own pizzas! Let them be creative.

**Top the Pizzas:** Brush olive oil (if using) around the rim of a crust. This is a great way to help the crust brown nicely and ensure that it is flavorful and gets eaten. Ladle crushed tomatoes into the center and spread in a circular motion over the surface of the crust. Be sparing, as too much sauce tends to make the crust a bit too wet and not bake well. Sprinkle with mozzarella and basil (if using), then drop small teaspoons of pesto (if using) all over. Repeat with the remaining dough rounds.

**Bake:** Use a pizza peel or a cutting board to carefully transfer the parchment and pizza onto the pizza stone or baking sheet. Bake one pizza at a time for 12 to 18 minutes, until the crust is browned and the cheese is melted. Oven temperatures can vary widely, so you may have to stay close by your pizza and keep an eye on it until you get accustomed to your oven. To pull the pizza out of the oven, simply slide the peel back under the pizza.

Pizza can be cut while hot and eaten as soon as you can tolerate it. The pizza cutter works best when used with a forceful and decisive motion, avoiding too much back and forth with the wheel of the cutter.

## Mortar and Pestle Pesto

Making pesto in a mortar and pestle is incredibly fun for kids and makes a nicer pesto, but you can whizz it through the blender or food processor if necessary. Traditional pesto is made with pine nuts, which can be quite expensive, but you can make pesto with walnuts for a thrifty and tasty alternative.

**Makes about 2 cups (230 g)**

| INGREDIENT | WEIGHT | VOLUME |
|---|---|---|
| Garlic | | 2 cloves |
| Raw walnuts | 30 g | ¼ cup |
| Fresh basil leaves | 40 g | 2 packed cups |
| Olive oil | 100 g | ½ cup, plus more for storage |
| Parmesan cheese, finely grated | 50 g | ½ cup |
| Pinch of salt, or to taste | | |

Using a mortar and pestle, pound the garlic until it becomes a paste, then add the walnuts and pound until creamy. Roughly chop the basil, then pound it into the paste. Drizzle in the olive oil while continuing to pound the mixture. When all the ingredients have come together, stir in the Parmesan cheese and add salt to taste.

Store the pesto in an airtight container in the fridge for about a week. Pouring a little olive oil over the top of the pesto will keep it fresh longer.

# Summer Bread Salad (Panzanella)

This classic Italian salad is perfect for kids because it is predominantly croutons. The fresh tomato and cucumber are cooling on a hot day, while the delicious toasty bread adds sustenance.

*Serves 4 to 6*

| INGREDIENT | WEIGHT | VOLUME |
|---|---|---|
| Cherry tomatoes, halved | 300 g | 2 pints |
| Cucumbers, peeled and sliced | | 2 medium |
| Handful of fresh basil, torn | | |
| Fine salt | 5 g | 1 teaspoon |
| All-Year Herb Croutons (page 92) | | |
| Gabe's Vinaigrette (recipe follows) | | |

In a large salad bowl, combine the tomatoes, cucumbers, and basil. Season with the salt and toss. Add the croutons, drizzle the vinaigrette over until it coats the salad evenly, and toss. Let the salad sit for about 20 minutes, so the flavors can combine.

The salad will keep for up to 1 day in an airtight container in the fridge, but the quality of the bread determines how well the croutons hold up (they may get soggy).

## Gabe's Vinaigrette

This is my 10-year-old son's favorite salad dressing. Start here and allow your kid to adjust the recipe until they land on their own creation; it's a great way for them to learn the flavors they like.

*Makes about ½ cup (120 g)*

| INGREDIENT | WEIGHT | VOLUME |
|---|---|---|
| Red wine vinegar | 10 g | 2 teaspoons |
| Juice of 1 lemon | 30 g | about 2 tablespoons |
| Honey (or any liquid sweetener you like) | 20 g | 1 tablespoon |
| Salt | 3 g | ½ teaspoon |
| Freshly ground black pepper | 3 g | ½ teaspoon |
| Mild-flavored olive oil | 50 g | ¼ cup |

In a small bowl, combine the vinegar, lemon juice, honey, salt, and pepper. Whisk well as you drizzle in the olive oil in a steady stream. Taste the dressing and adjust as needed. You can dress any salad with this—but don't forget the croutons (page 92)!

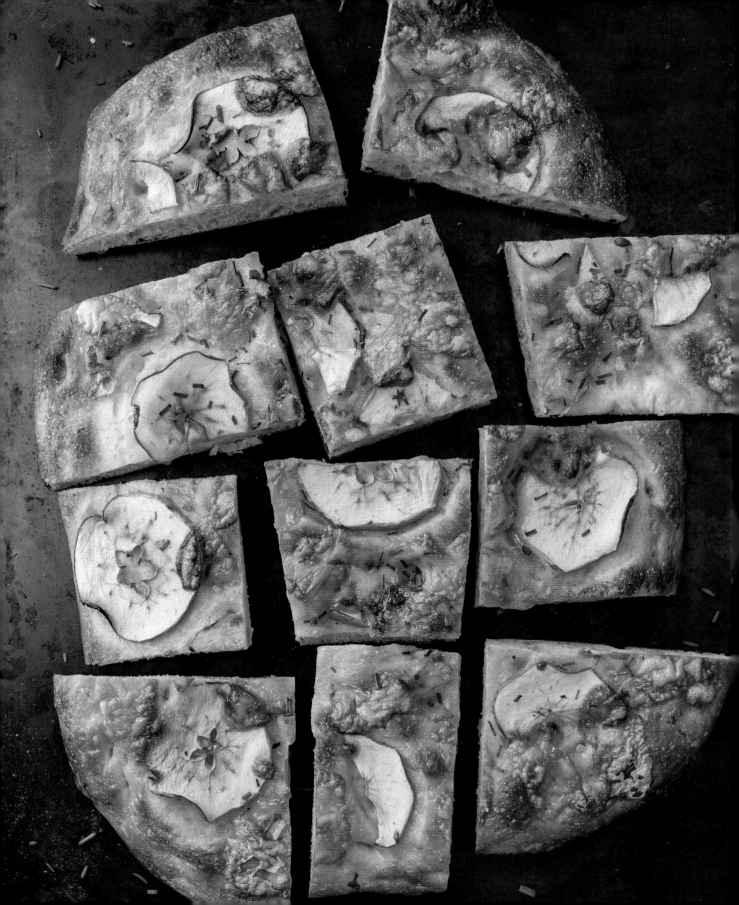

# Fall Focaccia with Apples, Pecans, and Cheddar

A favorite fall tradition for us is a visit to the apple orchards outside our town. This fluffy focaccia is a savory celebration of things we like to eat with apples, like Cheddar and pecans. It's like making a cheeseboard on top of fluffy bread. **Makes 1 focaccia**

| INGREDIENT | WEIGHT | VOLUME |
|---|---|---|
| 1 recipe focaccia dough (page 94) | | |
| **For the Toppings:** | | |
| Pecan halves or pieces | 114 g | 1 cup |
| Pure maple syrup | 40 g | 2 tablespoons |
| Apples, peeled, cored, and thinly sliced | 454 g | 1 pound or about 3 apples |
| Chives (or other fresh herbs of your choice), finely chopped | 6 g | 2 tablespoons |
| Aged Cheddar cheese | 250 g | 8 ounces |

**Prepare:** Weigh or measure all the ingredients and gather your supplies. Follow the recipe for the focaccia (page 94) through the Shape stage so that you have a flat, roughly 8 by 11-inch (20 by 27 cm) rectangle.

**Preheat:** Preheat the oven to 425°F (220°C).

**Candy the Pecans:** Line a baking sheet with parchment paper. In a bowl, toss the pecans with maple syrup and spread them out on the prepared sheet. Bake for 10 minutes, checking frequently to ensure they don't burn. Let cool.

**Top the Focaccia:** Press the candied pecans into the focaccia dough. Arrange the apple slices all over the dough, gently pressing them down into the surface. Sprinkle the herbs all over. Grate the Cheddar cheese all over the dough.

**Proof:** Let the focaccia proof, uncovered, at room temperature on the sheet pan used to shape the dough, for about 30 minutes.

**Bake:** Bake at 425°F (220°C) for 25 to 30 minutes, until the focaccia has a deep golden-brown crust and the cheese is bronzed. Check the focaccia halfway through the bake time and rotate the pan for a more even bake.

**Cool:** Let the focaccia cool on the pan for 20 to 30 minutes before slicing to maintain the fluffy crumb structure. Enjoy in the autumn sun, preferably with apple juice—and apple cider for grown-ups!

The large surface area of this bread makes it go stale quickly, so it's best when eaten within 2 days. Cut it into squares and store in a resealable plastic bag to keep soft.

## apple exploration

When apple season rolls around, visit an apple orchard, find a cidery, or just buy apples at your local market. Taste of all the different varieties available and see what you each like best. Compare, contrast, and rank your favorites! Some of ours are Ginger Gold, Empire, and Pink Lady. Don't forget to make a note of your favorites in your notebook!

# Fall Flatbread with Potatoes and Brussels Sprouts

In the fall, as tomatoes wane out of season and tiny Brussels sprouts start to show up at the farmers' market, we like to make this crispy pizza-style flatbread. Because the potatoes are a carbohydrate, I like to make this as a thin, crispy bread instead of a thick, fluffy one. The flatbread is based on the same dough (page 89) featured throughout this chapter, but it's pressed out more for a cracker-like crust. **Makes 1 flatbread**

| INGREDIENT | WEIGHT | VOLUME |
| --- | --- | --- |
| 1 recipe focaccia dough (page 94) | | |
| Yukon Gold potatoes, scrubbed and thinly sliced | 1 kg | 2 pounds or 4 medium potatoes |
| Fine salt | 12 g | 2 teaspoons |
| Brussels sprouts, thinly sliced | 115 g | 4 ounces or 10 to 12 small sprouts |
| Shallot, thinly sliced | 35 g | 1 medium |
| Olive oil | 25 g | 2 tablespoons, plus more for the pan |
| Roasted Garlic (optional; recipe follows) | | 4 cloves |
| Rosemary, finely chopped | 9 g | 1 tablespoon |
| Freshly ground black pepper | 3 g | ½ teaspoon |
| Prosciutto, thinly sliced | | about 4 slices |
| Parmesan cheese, shaved | 25 g | ¼ cup |

I like to use a vegetable peeler to make the Parmesan slivers, which kids can easily handle.

**Prepare:** Weigh or measure all the ingredients and gather your supplies. Follow the recipe for the focaccia (page 94) through the Rise stage. Place the sliced potatoes in a large bowl. Sprinkle the potatoes all over with about a teaspoon of the salt to draw out their moisture. Set them aside to rest while the dough rises for 90 minutes.

**Preheat:** Preheat the oven to 450°F (230°C).

**Shape:** Drizzle a half-sheet pan with an even coating of oil to prevent the dough from sticking. Scrape the dough out of the bowl onto a lightly floured work surface. Gently stretch the dough into a rectangle not quite as large as your pan. Stretch by gently picking up the dough, holding it over your fists, and letting gravity gently stretch the dough. If the dough feels like it cannot stretch further, let it rest for 10 minutes, covered with a kitchen towel, before trying again. When you have a flat, roughly 8 by 11-inch (20 by 27 cm) rectangle, you're ready to add the toppings. Transfer the stretched dough to the prepared pan. Press with your fingers to coax the dough into all the corners of the pan.

**Top:** Drain any excess water from the potatoes, squeezing them in a kitchen towel if necessary. Add the Brussels sprouts, shallot, olive oil, roasted garlic (if using), rosemary, remaining 1 teaspoon salt, and pepper to the bowl with the potatoes and toss. Have kids help evenly distribute the toppings all over the focaccia dough. Top with the prosciutto and Parmesan.

continued

**Bake:** Bake for 25 to 30 minutes, until the crust is deep brown and crispy and the potato edges have started to caramelize and brown. Check the flatbread halfway through the bake time and rotate the pan for a more even bake.

While green vegetables can be polarizing, Brussels sprouts are some of the most approachable for kids.

This flatbread should be eaten the same day you bake it.

# Roasted Garlic

Roasted garlic is incredible spread across fresh bread or as a topping for pizza or focaccia.

*Makes 1 head of roasted garlic*

| INGREDIENT | WEIGHT | VOLUME |
|---|---|---|
| Garlic | | 1 head |
| Olive oil | 25 g | 2 tablespoons, plus more for storage |

Preheat the oven to 400°F (200°C).

Use a knife to cut the top off the garlic head. Place the garlic on a large sheet of aluminum foil, drizzle the olive oil over the garlic, and then wrap it tightly in the foil.

Roast the garlic in its foil packet for 30 to 40 minutes. Use tongs to remove the packet from the oven. Being careful to avoid dripping any hot oil, take a peek inside. The garlic should be soft, with a beautiful, deep golden-brown color.

Let the garlic cool completely, then use a butter knife to pop the soft cloves out of the papery skins. Store in an airtight container in the fridge for about a week, covered in oil to keep them soft.

# Fall Herbs Crackers

The combination of parsley, sage, rosemary, and thyme can be nostalgic. These hardy herbs are incorporated into a lot of savory items associated with cooler weather, like roast chicken or turkey, seasonal stuffing, and beautiful soups. Picking and plucking these herbs is a great hands-on activity to do with kids. Once they're acquainted with rosemary and its distinct aroma, they will begin to notice how often it can be found in the world around them, as it's often incorporated into all kinds of landscaping.

**Makes about 50 crackers, depending on the size of your crackers**

| INGREDIENT | WEIGHT | VOLUME |
| --- | --- | --- |
| All-purpose flour | 200 g | 1⅔ cups |
| Whole wheat flour | 100 g | ¾ cup plus 2 tablespoons |
| Water | 120 g | ½ cup, plus more as needed |
| Unsalted butter, melted and cooled | 30 g | 2 tablespoons |
| Sugar | 16 g | 1 rounded tablespoon |
| Salt | 5 g | 1 scant teaspoon |
| Fresh flat-leaf parsley, chopped | 7 g | ¼ cup |
| Fresh sage, chopped | 4 g | 2 tablespoons |
| Fresh rosemary, chopped | 7 g | 1 tablespoon |
| Fresh thyme leaves | 2 g | 1 tablespoon |
| Olive oil, for brushing | | |
| Flaky sea salt | | |

**Prepare:** Weigh or measure all the ingredients and gather your supplies.

**Mix:** In a large bowl, combine both flours with the water, butter, sugar, salt, parsley, sage, rosemary, and thyme. Mix by hand until you have a smooth dough. This dough will be much stiffer than most bread dough. It should be firm and not sticky, but not too dry either. If there is dry flour left in your bowl, add water, 1 teaspoon at a time, until the dough comes together.

**Knead:** Turn the dough out onto a lightly floured work surface. If the dough feels sticky or tacky, dust with small amounts of flour to adjust the consistency while kneading. Knead the dough with a push-and-fold motion. Firmly push the dough away from you, then fold it back toward you, rotating the dough a quarter turn every few folds. Repeat pushing and folding for about 5 minutes, or until the dough feels smooth, tight, and bouncy.

**Rest:** This dough doesn't need to rise at all, but it does need to rest to make it easier to roll out. Wrap in plastic wrap or beeswax wrap. If you want to make crackers as soon as possible, you can let the dough rest for 30 minutes at room temperature. If you want to make the crackers later, you can rest the dough in the fridge for up to 4 days.

continued

## fall herbs crackers, continued

**Preheat:** Preheat the oven to 375°F (190°C).

**Roll:** On a lightly floured work surface, use a lightly floured rolling pin to roll the dough out as thin as possible into a large square (roughly 12 by 12 inches/30 by 30 cm; perfectionism is not necessary here). Make sure the dough isn't sticking to the work surface by lifting it up and dusting a bit of flour underneath for good measure. Gently roll the dough a bit further to make sure it has a roughly even thickness.

**Shape:** Line 2 sheet pans with parchment paper. Use cookie cutters to cut the crackers into fun shapes or a pizza cutter to cut them into squares or diamonds. A fluted ravioli/pasta cutter and a ruler can help you cut diamond shapes, giving the crackers a professional, boxed cracker appearance. Place the shaped crackers on the prepared pans. The crackers don't expand at all, so you can put them really close together.

Be creative and experiment with cutting the crackers into different kinds of fall leaf shapes, harmonious with the herbs incorporated within.

**Finish:** Brush the crackers with olive oil and sprinkle with flaky sea salt.

**Bake:** The crackers bake quickly. Bake for 14 to 18 minutes, until the crackers are medium golden brown, or a bit darker, depending on your preference. Peek halfway through the bake time and switch the placement of the sheet pans and rotate them for a more even bake.

**Cool:** Transfer the crackers to a wire rack to keep them crispy.

The crackers will keep in an airtight container for about a week.

# Caramelized Onion Dip

Much like roasting garlic (see page 126), this is a simple task with a huge flavor payoff, and dancing in the kitchen while stirring onions is a great way to hang out. The rest of the work is just a matter of combining ingredients!

**Makes 2 cups (450 g)**

| INGREDIENT | WEIGHT | VOLUME |
|---|---|---|
| Unsalted butter | 30 g | 2 tablespoons |
| Onions, diced | 340 g | 2 medium onions |
| Fresh thyme leaves | 2 g | 1 tablespoon |
| Sour cream | 340 g | 1½ cups |
| Chives, finely chopped | 9 g | 3 tablespoons |
| Juice of 1 lemon | | |
| Salt and freshly ground black pepper | | |

**Caramelize the Onions:** In a medium skillet over low-medium heat, melt the butter. Add the onions and thyme and cook, gently stirring, for about 35 minutes, or until the onions are glossy and deeply golden brown. If at any point in the process you feel like they are getting too dry or sticking to the skillet, you can drop in a tablespoon or two of water and continue with stirring. When the onions are done cooking, transfer them to a mixing bowl and set aside to cool.

Teaching kids how to caramelize onions is a noble pursuit! It takes about 30 minutes, so if you have a young person who needs to exercise their patience a bit, this might be just the thing. Put on some tunes and have some quality time with a wooden spoon together.

**Make the Dip:** When the onions have cooled, add the sour cream, chives, and lemon juice and stir gently. Season with salt and pepper to taste. Store in the fridge for an hour (or more) to help the flavors meld. You can always make the dip a few days ahead and store it in an airtight container in the fridge.

# Winter Olive and Lemon Focaccia

Citrus is in season during the winter months, and a bread dimpled generously with Meyer lemon zest and Castelvetrano olives (or any olives your child likes) can be a bright spot in a cold winter day.

*Makes 1 focaccia*

| INGREDIENT | WEIGHT | VOLUME |
|---|---|---|
| Olive oil, for the pan | | |
| 1 recipe focaccia dough (page 94) | | |
| **For the Toppings:** | | |
| Green olives, pitted | 150 g | 1 cup, drained |
| Finely grated zest of 2 lemons | | |
| Fresh thyme leaves | 2 g | 1 tablespoon |

**Prepare:** Weigh or measure all the ingredients and gather your supplies. Follow the recipe for the focaccia (page 94) through the Rise stage. In a small bowl, toss the olives, lemon zest, and thyme. Let the flavors meld for a few minutes.

**Preheat:** Preheat the oven to 425°F (220°C).

**Shape:** Drizzle a half-sheet pan with an even coating of olive oil to prevent the dough from sticking. Scrape the dough out of the bowl onto the prepared sheet pan in one large piece. Gently stretch the dough into a rectangle, not quite as large as the pan. Stretch by gently picking up the dough, holding it over your fists, and letting gravity gently stretch the dough. If the dough feels like it cannot stretch further, let it rest on the counter for 10 minutes, covered with a kitchen towel, before trying again. When you have a flat, roughly 8 by 11-inch (20 by 27 cm) rectangle, you're ready to add the toppings.

**Top the Focaccia:** Scatter the olive mixture over the dough, pressing the olives in gently to keep them from rolling off as the dough expands in the oven.

**Bake:** Bake for 25 to 30 minutes, until the focaccia is golden brown and crisp. Check the focaccia halfway through the bake time and rotate the pan for a more even bake.

**Cool:** Let the focaccia cool on the pan for 20 to 30 minutes before slicing to maintain the fluffy crumb structure.

The large surface area of this bread makes it go stale quickly, so it's best when eaten within 2 days. Cut into squares and store in a resealable plastic bag to keep soft.

>>> turn the page for a tart and refreshing drink!

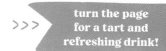

# >>> Gabe's Lemonade

My son Gabe has spent more time making lemonade than most people; it's something he takes a lot of pride in. He's generally a reserved person, so if he quietly offers you a glass of his lemonade, you know he's fond of you. This lemonade has a ratio of 4:2:1 for water, sugar syrup, and lemon juice, which is both straightforward and easy to remember. Meyer lemons taste a bit more floral and sweeter than regular lemons, but regular ones will work for this recipe, too.

*Makes 7 cups (1.7 L)*

| INGREDIENT | WEIGHT | VOLUME |
|---|---|---|
| **For the Simple Syrup:** | | |
| Sugar | 200 g | 1 cup |
| Boiling water | 240 g | 1 cup |
| **For the Lemonade:** | | |
| Lemon juice | 227 g | 1 cup or juice of 5 to 6 lemons |
| Cold water | 960 g | 4 cups |

**Make the Simple Syrup:** Place the sugar in a clear Pyrex liter (4 cup) measuring cup. Place the cup on a flat surface, then pour in the boiling water up to the 500 ml (2 cup) mark. Stir gently with a long spoon until all the sugar has dissolved. You can also do this in a saucepan if you don't have a sturdy Pyrex measuring cup.

**Make the Lemonade:** In a large pitcher, combine the lemon juice, cold water, and simple syrup and stir well. Keep the lemonade in the fridge and serve over ice. Cheers!

You can tinker with this recipe until you arrive at your own ideal combination of tartness and sweetness (it's a balance!). Don't forget to write down your own perfect formula!

### citrus and herbs scavenger hunt

Take a walk around your neighborhood together and keep an eye out for edible plants! How many fruit or citrus trees do you see? Do you see a garden with a hardy rosemary plant? These strolls offer great opportunities for chatting with neighbors. Most people who have mature fruit trees have trouble dealing with all the fruit when it's ripe and are happy to share. The same goes for herbs, which can be prolific and take over a whole garden. Bonus points if you bring a loaf of bread to your neighbors when you ask for a fruit-and-herbs trade!

# Sweet Potato and Orange Zest Fougasse

On a cold night, you can roast a big tray of sweet potatoes for dinner and set some aside for making this bread. If you don't have time to roast the sweet potatoes, you can always use canned sweet potato puree or even pumpkin; both will impart the warm gold color and mild sweetness to this dough. Fougasse is typically shaped like a leaf, but this version is shaped to look like little ocher-colored flames to warm your belly in the dead of winter.

*Makes 1 fougasse*

| INGREDIENT | WEIGHT | VOLUME |
|---|---|---|
| Water | 200 g | ¾ cup plus 2 tablespoons |
| Instant yeast | 7 g | 2½ teaspoons |
| All-purpose flour | 200 g | 1⅔ cups |
| Whole wheat flour | 200 g | 1⅔ cups |
| Roasted sweet potato or squash, mashed or pureed | 100 g | scant ½ cup |
| Fine salt | 8 g | 1 rounded teaspoon |
| Olive oil, for the pan | | |
| **For the Topping:** | | |
| Olive oil | 50 g | ¼ cup |
| Finely grated zest of 1 large or 2 small oranges | | |
| Fresh sage, finely chopped | | |
| Flaky sea salt (optional) | | |

**Prepare:** Use the temperature chart (see page 27) to prepare the water to the correct temperature. Keep in mind that on cooler days (below 75°F/23°C) the dough may take a bit longer to rise. On warmer days (above 75°F/23°C) the dough may rise more quickly. Weigh or measure all the ingredients and gather your supplies.

**Mix:** In a large bowl, combine the water and yeast by swishing it around with your fingers until well dissolved. Add both flours and the sweet potato, then the salt. Mix by hand, using a grab-and-squish motion to thoroughly combine all the ingredients. Alternatively, use a wooden spoon to mix. The dough is well mixed when it is smooth and there are no dry bits of flour. This may take about 5 minutes.

**Fold:** Bring the dough together with folds. Starting on the side of the bowl closest to you, scoop both hands under the sides of the dough and glide your hands around the perimeter of the bowl, each hand moving on one side in a semicircular motion, gently stretching the dough away from you as you go. Once your hands meet again at the top of the bowl, pull the dough over itself, across the bowl, back toward you. Work like this around the bowl until the dough forms a tight ball.

**Rise:** Cover the bowl with a kitchen towel (or plastic wrap, if necessary, in drier climates), and let rise for 45 minutes.

*continued*

## sweet potato and orange zest fougasse, continued

To create the shape, you may need to help your child press down hard enough to cut through the dough and gently pull the slashes open. It's not important for it to be perfect—every fougasse you make will be a unique expression.

**Prepare the Topping:** While the dough is rising, combine the olive oil, orange zest, and sage in a bowl to infuse. Set aside.

**Preheat:** Preheat the oven to 425°F (220°C).

**Shape:** Drizzle a half-sheet pan with an even coating of olive oil to prevent the dough from sticking. Scrape the dough out of the bowl onto the prepared pan in one large piece. Gently stretch the dough into a soft triangle or pear shape, not quite as large as the pan. Stretch by gently picking up the dough, holding it over your fists, and letting gravity gently stretch the dough. If the dough feels like it cannot stretch further, let it rest on the counter for 10 minutes, covered with a kitchen towel, before trying again. To even out the dough, dimple it gently with your fingers, pressing with fingertips all over the dough. Use a pizza cutter and press down firmly to cut slashes into the dough. I usually do one cut in the center and three on each side (as pictured on page 135), but you can use your creativity. Gently pull the bread to open the slashes and create the flame shape.

**Top the Fougasse:** Use a pastry brush to brush the dough with the infused oil. Sprinkle pinches of flaky salt over the top of the dough, if desired.

**Bake:** Bake for 18 to 24 minutes, until deep golden brown. Check the fougasse halfway through the bake time and rotate the pan for a more even bake.

**Cool:** Let the fougasse cool on the pan for about 15 minutes and eat as soon as possible.

I don't recommend extended storage of this bread—it's best enjoyed the same day, hopefully torn by hand around a table and dipped in dukkah (recipe follows) for maximum flavor and warmth in the dead of winter.

# Central Valley Dukkah

Duqqa, or dukkah, is an Egyptian and Middle Eastern condiment made from a mixture of herbs, nuts, and spices. The word *duqqa* means "to pound," as it is made in a mortar and pestle. Traditionally, it contains hazelnuts, but the Central Valley of California (where I live) is the almond capital of the world and we are surrounded by almond orchards, so here we make dukkah with almonds.

**Makes about 1 cup (200 g)**

| INGREDIENT | WEIGHT | VOLUME |
|---|---|---|
| Sesame seeds | 35 g | ¼ cup |
| Fennel seeds | 6 g | 3 teaspoons |
| Coriander seeds | 4 g | 2 teaspoons |
| Cumin seeds | 2 g | 1 teaspoon |
| Anise seeds | 2 g | 1 teaspoon |
| Almonds, roasted | 142 g | 1 cup |
| Fine salt | 6 g | 1 teaspoon |
| Freshly ground black pepper | 3 g | 1 teaspoon |

**Toast the Spices:** Heat a skillet over medium-low heat. Add the sesame seeds and use a wooden spoon or spatula to stir them continuously for about 60 seconds, or until they smell nutty, then slide them out of the pan and into the mortar. Repeat with the fennel, coriander, cumin, and anise, toasting each of the spices individually, stirring them until they become fragrant, then removing them one after the other into the mortar.

 Buy pre-roasted nuts to make this more quickly, or roast almonds yourself (see Almond Butter, page 54).

**Pound the Dukkah:** Use the mortar and pestle to crush the almonds with the seeds. You don't want to pound so much that it becomes a paste; you're looking for a crunchy consistency. Season with salt and pepper and stir together. You can keep this in a jar at room temperature for a few weeks.

# Breads Around the World

RECIPES EXPLORING HISTORY AND CULTURE,
FOR AGES 12 TO 14

## In This Chapter

* **Working with different kinds of grains**
* **Rolling out flatbreads**
* **Cooking flatbreads on a stove top**

Bread is central to the history of civilization. The study of bread and other foods reveals much to us about the culture, politics, and values of past societies. Through baking bread, we can bring history to life and connect to the humanity and stories of those who came before us.

These global bread recipes travel through time and region, covering a range of dough types that incorporate a diversity of grains and flours. When we say the word *bread*, what may first come to mind is the wrapped and sliced loaf at the grocery store, but bread has taken many forms throughout history, and some look nothing like today's grocery store breads—take a delicate lentil cake (page 163) or crisp crackerbread (page 147), for example.

Across the globe, foods tend to cross-pollinate. A bread from one region might also be made in another region, but perhaps with a different name or a slightly different shape, ingredients, or process. This chapter features a variety of flatbreads, like soft corn and wheat tortillas (page 149), tender pitas with pockets for fillings (page 155), and fluffy naan (page 158) brushed with garlic butter (page 161). Kids can build off their experience making lean and enriched doughs with breads that incorporate potatoes (page 173), rye and corn (page 171), and even apple cider (page 164).

# Learning Opportunities

Middle school kids are ready to be more independent bakers. Encourage your child to read these recipes on their own, taking note of the prompts and sidebars to pursue deeper information. The learning opportunities presented by a global approach to bread baking will reflect the topics kids are likely encountering in school, with a focus on the following concepts.

## Interpreting History

Bread can tell us a lot about ancient cultures. What we know about foods from ancient times comes from artistic renderings (like Egyptian tomb drawings), literature (poems, folklore, religious writings), and archaeological evidence (ruins, grinding stones, ancient tools).

## Piecing Together a Timeline

Typically, we learn about world history in pieces, studying different civilizations and time periods separately. In reality, food, literature, politics, religion, and culture are interwoven through time and space. Following these threads via a single type of food like bread helps create a more cohesive mental map that is easier for kids to digest.

## Making Connections

Bread may take on different names, but almost everyone eats the same collection of grains. Discovering the similarities of the breads from different traditions is a reminder that however different cultures may seem on the surface, we have a lot in common.

## Working Together

Recipes that are a bit more labor-intensive are best made through teamwork, with friends or family. It's an apt depiction of the work required to make foods before industrialization. Oftentimes the work was shared, especially among groups of women. Grinding grains by hand or with tools, mixing large batches of dough by hand, and shaping and firing flatbreads would have been a communal activity that would take all day.

# The History of Bread

This timeline is constructed with approximated dates to give you a big-picture overview of bread through the ages and across the world.

**Around 10,000 BCE:** The first signs of early varieties of wheat like emmer and einkorn and grain domestication appear in the Fertile Crescent, a region in the Middle East spanning modern-day Iraq, Syria, Lebanon, Palestine, Israel, Jordan, and northern Egypt.

**4000–3000 BCE:** Egyptians discover natural leavening and create the first leavened breads, called aish baladi, which are similar to today's pitas. Egyptians also create the first ovens and bread molds and domesticate and farm wheat on a massive and organized scale.

**200 BCE:** Romans use teams of animals or enslaved people to turn millstones and grind flour in great quantities, the first baker's guild is formed, and bread baking becomes a recognized profession integral to the structure of society. The Romans make breads called panis focacius (from the Latin *focus*, "hearth"), an early version of the breads now known as focaccia.

**6500–5500 BCE:** The cultivation of emmer, an early form of wheat, reaches ancient Greece. Goddesses, temples, and rituals are devoted to wheat cultivation. Millstones for grinding flour are invented.

**1500 BCE–200 CE:** The formation and endurance of Judeo-Christian religion during this time can be directly correlated to the proliferation of bread. People hunger greatly for bread and make it using many kinds of grains and legumes. (*Bethlehem* means "house of bread"; God sends manna, or bread, to fall from heaven; there are prayers for daily bread; Jesus multiplies bread to feed a crowd as a miracle; Jesus says, "I am the bread of life.")

**800–1500 CE:** Vikings eat a diet of mostly whole-meal bread made from rye and oats. Throughout Europe, the basic diet of the medieval peasant consists of carbohydrates in the form of grains, mostly barley and oats, which are baked or brewed into bread and ales. People use old hollowed-out bread as bowls, called trenchers.

**1760s–1790s:** Wheat and bread play a vital role in the American Revolutionary War. Entire bakeries are commissioned to bake for soldiers, and cutting off the food supply for enemies is a military strategy. At this same time, the budding French Revolution is fueled by a lack of bread for peasants. Queen Marie Antoinette is notoriously guillotined for recommending that they eat brioche instead.

**Unknown–1500:** Spanish missionaries arrive in the Americas with the voyages of Columbus, bringing wheat with them. Indigenous inhabitants of Mesoamerica primarily eat maize bread, which the Spanish call *tortilla*, meaning "little cake." This word relates back to southern Spain, where flatbreads had been previously introduced from the Middle East. Over a long period of time, wheat products start to become more prevalent than corn in the Americas.

**1800s–1928:** A massive industrial revolution takes place in Europe and North America. Railroads, large-scale wheat farms, gasoline-fueled tractors, chemical fertilizers, industrial roller mills, and baking-specific machinery all come together to create a modern marvel: enriched sliced white bread. Presliced loaves hit the market in 1928 and are heralded as "the greatest forward step in the baking industry since bread was wrapped."

**1600:** The potato arrives in Europe from South America and is cultivated famously well in Ireland. European breads that incorporate what they call "floury potatoes" become numerous. Around the same time, wheat arrives in South America, and people in Brazil and Chile make breads using a combination of wheat and potatoes, too.

**1940–Today:** Smaller artisanal baking companies begin building a network of high-quality neighborhood bakeries, local-grain economies, and small local mills. New cookbooks about using a diverse array of whole grains are being published, and home bakers are learning to mill their own flour and bake bread products of all kinds with heirloom and whole grains. A huge boom and interest in home bread baking and sourdough baking bring back the desire for homemade bread.

**1830s–1940s:** Reverend Sylvester Graham and his follower Doctor John Harvey Kellogg promote a plant-based diet of whole grains and high-fiber foods for health and wellness.

# Crackerbread

The origins of bread as we know it began with something more like a cracker in the Neolithic-era Middle East, before agriculture became a way of life and the art of leavening was discovered. An unleavened bread still eaten today is matzoh, an important part of Jewish culture that predates the Bible. Another example is a Persian bread called sangak, which is a large, thin flatbread cooked over fire-heated river rocks. In India and Africa, you'll find chapatis. Crackerlike flatbreads, whatever the name, are convenient and portable, and they can be flavored with seeds and spices, too.

*Makes 4 cracker-style breads*

| INGREDIENT | WEIGHT | VOLUME |
|---|---|---|
| Whole oats | 20 g | ¼ cup |
| Whole spices, such as peppercorns, mustard seeds, cumin seeds, or coriander seeds (optional) | 4 g | 1 tablespoon |
| All-purpose flour | 200 g | 1⅔ cups |
| Water | 120 g | ½ cup |
| Fine salt | 4 g | ½ rounded teaspoon |

**Prepare:** Weigh or measure the ingredients and gather your supplies. In a blender or food processor, grind the oats and the spices, if using, until fine.

Archaeologists suggest that Neolithic peoples incorporated spices and seeds into their grain products. If you have a mortar and pestle, let your child grind the oats and spices by hand. The process will help them appreciate the convenience of buying flour and the hard physical labor of all the people who used to make bread by grinding the flour by hand.

**Mix:** In a large bowl, combine the ground oats and spices (if using), flour, water, and salt. Mix by hand, using a grab-and-squish motion to thoroughly combine all the ingredients, until the dough comes together in a smooth ball. This dough does not have a lot of water in it, so it should come together very quickly and be simple to work with.

**Knead:** Turn the dough out onto a lightly floured work surface. Knead the dough with a push-and-fold motion. Firmly push the dough away from you, then fold it back toward you, rotating the dough a quarter turn every few folds. Repeat pushing and folding for about 5 minutes, or until the dough is smooth and not sticky or tacky.

continued

## crackerbread, continued

You may have to adjust the heat a bit to find the right temperature for cooking the crackerbread. Have a conversation about how you think people cooking with fire adjusted temperatures while making breads. Do you ever cook with fire? Maybe roasting marshmallows while camping? How do these experiences relate to each other?

**Rest:** Return the dough to the bowl, cover with a kitchen towel (or plastic wrap, if necessary, in drier climates), and let it rest for 15 minutes.

**Divide and Shape:** Turn the dough out onto a lightly floured work surface. Divide the dough into 4 pieces, roughly 85 grams each. Using a rolling pin, roll each portion of dough out as thin as you can without tearing it. Use a fork to prick little holes all over the dough; this will allow it to cook more evenly.

**Cook:** Heat a 10-inch (25 cm) or larger skillet over medium-high heat. Gently stretch 1 portion of dough with your fingers as you pick it up, so the holes open slightly, then carefully lay it in the hot skillet.

Dip your fingers in a bowl of water and sprinkle lightly over the cracker dough, creating a gentle mist. Cook, flipping with a spatula or tongs, for about 2 minutes on each side, or until the cracker has little bubbles and scorch marks all over it. Repeat with the remaining pieces of dough.

Crackerbread is best when eaten the same day it is made. Eat while warm for flexible bread or allow to cool for more of a crunchy cracker. You can eat it plain or spread with goat cheese or herbs and a drizzle of olive oil.

# Corn and Wheat Tortillas

Masa harina is a flour made of nixtamalized corn and is commonly used to make corn tortillas. It is available in most grocery stores in the baking aisle. A commonly found brand is Maseca. These tortillas are made with a blend of corn and wheat so that they will be easier for you to make by hand—no need for a tortilla press—while retaining the flavor of the corn. Hold on to that masa harina to make Rye, Wheat, and Corn Bread (page 171).

Makes 4 tortillas

| INGREDIENT | WEIGHT | VOLUME |
| --- | --- | --- |
| Masa harina | 100 g | 1 cup plus 1 tablespoon |
| All-purpose flour | 100 g | ¾ cup plus 2 tablespoons |
| Water | 200 g | ¾ cup plus 2 tablespoons |
| Fine salt | 4 g | ½ rounded teaspoon |
| Cooking spray or neutral oil, for the pan | | |

**Prepare:** Weigh or measure the ingredients and gather your supplies.

**Mix:** In a large bowl, combine the masa harina, flour, water, and salt. Mix by hand, using a grab-and-squish motion to thoroughly combine all the ingredients, until the dough comes together in a smooth ball. This dough does not have a lot of water in it, so it should come together very quickly and be simple to work with.

**Knead:** Turn the dough out onto a lightly floured work surface. Knead the dough with a push-and-fold motion. Firmly push the dough away from you, then fold it back toward you, rotating the dough a quarter turn every few folds. Repeat pushing and folding for about 5 minutes, or until the dough is smooth and not sticky or tacky.

**Rest:** Return the dough to the bowl, cover it with a kitchen towel (or plastic wrap, if necessary, in drier climates), and let it rest for 30 minutes. This dough isn't yeasted and doesn't need to rise; it will just rest and relax a bit, making it easier to roll out.

**Divide and Shape:** Turn the dough out onto a lightly floured work surface. Divide the dough into 4 golf ball–size pieces, roughly 100 grams each. Use your hands to gently round each piece into a ball, then place them on your work surface. Keep the balls covered with a damp towel as you work to prevent them from drying out.

continued

## corn and wheat tortillas, continued

Rolling out the tortillas thinly and evenly takes a bit of practice—it's okay to take your time and go slowly. You can roll out all the tortillas at once and place them on parchment paper covered with a kitchen towel while they wait to be cooked, or you can take turns rolling and cooking with someone else.

Cooking tortillas is a good two-person job, because it goes much faster if one person cooks the tortillas and the other person rolls out the next tortilla. Take turns; both roles are active and rewarding.

To make tortillas, use a rolling pin to roll each dough ball out in all directions, making it as round as possible. (This will take practice and you'll get better with each try. If the dough sticks, add a little flour to your work surface.) You want each tortilla to be about 8 inches (20 cm) in diameter.

**Cook:** Heat a large, heavy skillet over medium-high heat. Mist the pan with cooking spray or carefully rub it with a bit of oil on a paper towel.

Place a tortilla in the hot skillet. Cook for 30 to 90 seconds on each side, or until you see little brown spots underneath or the tortilla puffs up a bit. When the tortilla is blistered on both sides, transfer to a plate and cover with a kitchen towel to keep soft.

Mist the pan again and continue frying the tortillas; you may have to reduce the heat, as the pan retains heat over the cooking time.

Tortillas are best eaten right away, while they are still soft. Spread with butter, fill with beans, or add cheese and make quesadillas. So satisfying.

### corn in the americas

Indigenous people in South America made flatbread from local corn; in North America, it was made with acorns, which were ground by hand with stone tools. The corn and acorns were ground on rocks or a metate, which is a large Mexican mortar-and-pestle-type tool. Corn must undergo a process called nixtamalization before it can be used to make tortillas, and acorns must also be processed in a way that leaches their tannins before they can be used to make flatbreads. All over the world, humans realized that they could eat grains by grinding and hydrating them into a thick porridge and shaping the dough to their will. This produced such beloved portable foods as tortillas, flatbreads, and crackers.

# Herb Sauce

Many different cultures enjoy a condiment made of finely chopped or pounded herbs. Like chimichurri, the popular herbaceous South American condiment, this tangy sauce goes with just about anything—drizzle it over savory fillings in your tortillas or pitas for a pop of brightness. It also resembles the Middle Eastern condiment zhoug, made of cilantro, parsley, and peppers.

Makes about 2 cups (275 g)

| INGREDIENT | WEIGHT | VOLUME |
|---|---|---|
| Garlic | | 3 cloves |
| Extra-virgin olive oil | 132 g | ⅔ cup |
| Red wine vinegar | 80 g | ⅓ cup |
| Fresh cilantro, finely chopped | 30 g | ½ cup |
| Fresh flat-leaf parsley, finely chopped | 15 g | ¼ cup |
| Pinch of salt | | |
| Pinch of red pepper flakes (optional) | | |

In a blender or food processor, combine the garlic, olive oil, vinegar, cilantro, and parsley and pulse a few times until finely chopped. Season with a pinch of salt and red pepper flakes, if desired. The sauce should not be pureed to a liquid; it should have small herb pieces in it. The herb sauce keeps in an airtight container in the fridge for a week.

corn and wheat tortillas, page 149

# Pita

Also known as aish baladi in Egypt, pita was cooked in some of the first ovens in history! This leavened flatbread is known by different names around the Middle East and Mediterranean. The Greeks incorporated olive oil into their breads, and the ancient Romans made panis focacius, bread that looked a bit like modern focaccia. Pita is now a common grocery store item; the little pockets make them a wonderful transportable food that can be filled with meat or vegetables and sauces for a school lunch or a lunch on the go.

Makes 6 pitas

| INGREDIENT | WEIGHT | VOLUME |
|---|---|---|
| All-purpose flour | 200 g | 1⅔ cups |
| Whole wheat flour | 100 g | ¾ cup plus 2 tablespoons |
| Water | 180 g | ¾ cup |
| Olive oil | 5 g | 1 teaspoon, plus more for the pan |
| Instant yeast | 2 g | scant ½ teaspoon |
| Fine salt | 6 g | 1 teaspoon |
| Neutral oil, for the pan | | |

**Prepare:** Weigh or measure the ingredients and gather your supplies.

**Mix:** In a large bowl, combine both flours with the water, olive oil, yeast, and salt. Mix by hand, using a grab-and-squish motion to thoroughly combine all the ingredients, until the dough comes together in a smooth ball.

**Knead:** Turn the dough out onto a lightly floured work surface. Knead the dough with a push-and-fold motion. Firmly push the dough away from you, then fold it back toward you, rotating the dough a quarter turn every few folds. Repeat pushing and folding for about 5 minutes, or until the dough is smooth and not sticky or tacky.

**Rise:** Return the dough to the bowl, cover it with a kitchen towel (or plastic wrap, if necessary, in drier climates), and let rise in a warm place for 60 minutes. It will puff slightly, but this is a flatbread so the dough will not rise significantly.

**Divide and Shape:** Turn the dough out onto a lightly floured work surface. Divide the dough into 6 pieces, roughly 80 grams each. Use your hands to gently round each piece into a ball, then place them on your work surface. Cover the balls with a kitchen towel and let them rest for 20 minutes.

continued

## pita, continued

Don't be afraid to take your time rolling the pitas. They puff best when they are evenly rolled and a bit thin. With practice, each one will turn out better than the previous one! →

Cooking the pita in a pan with a glass lid contains the heat around the dough, so it cooks all the way through and allows you to watch the pita puff up.

It may take a few tries to get the heat just right; you want it to be hot enough to puff the bread without scorching it.

To make pitas, use a rolling pin to roll each dough ball out in all directions, making it as round as possible. You want each pita to be about 6 inches (15 cm) in diameter. Dust the surface of the pita with a little flour if the dough sticks.

**Cook:** Heat a large skillet with a glass lid over medium-high heat and lightly grease the pan with neutral oil.

Place a pita in the heated pan and cover with the lid. After 45 to 60 seconds, the pita will expand like a big bubble!

Remove the lid, flip the puffed pita with tongs or a spatula, and cook on the other side for about a minute longer. If your pita didn't expand evenly, try rolling the next one more evenly. Keep rolling and cooking pitas until they are all cooked, wrapping them in a kitchen towel to keep them soft while you work.

To eat, fill the puffed pita pocket with savory ingredients. Store cooled pitas in a resealable plastic bag; they will keep for a few days.

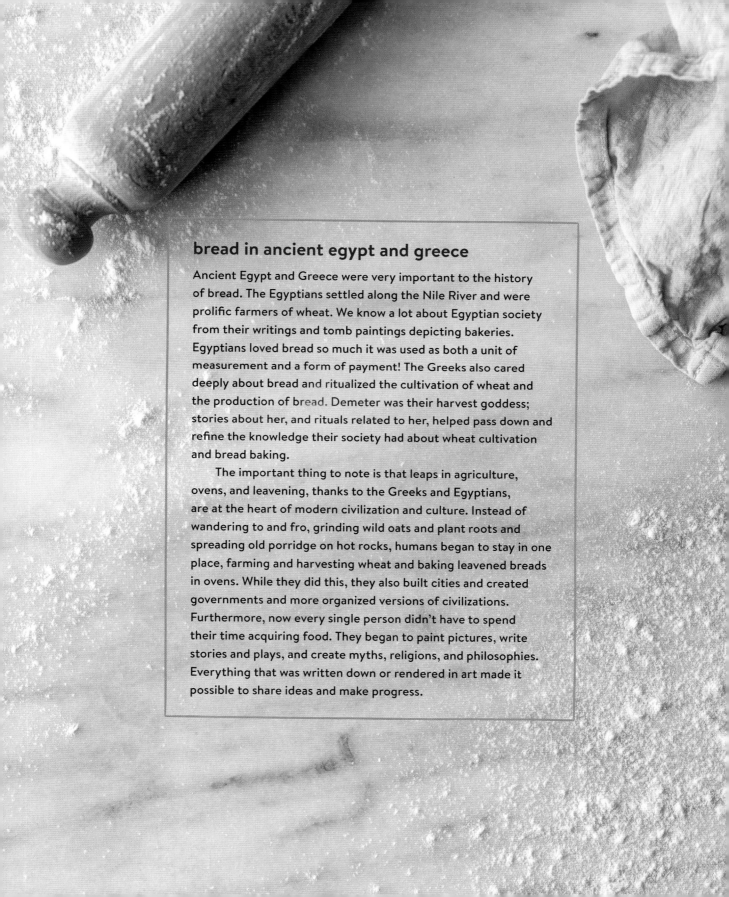

## bread in ancient egypt and greece

Ancient Egypt and Greece were very important to the history of bread. The Egyptians settled along the Nile River and were prolific farmers of wheat. We know a lot about Egyptian society from their writings and tomb paintings depicting bakeries. Egyptians loved bread so much it was used as both a unit of measurement and a form of payment! The Greeks also cared deeply about bread and ritualized the cultivation of wheat and the production of bread. Demeter was their harvest goddess; stories about her, and rituals related to her, helped pass down and refine the knowledge their society had about wheat cultivation and bread baking.

The important thing to note is that leaps in agriculture, ovens, and leavening, thanks to the Greeks and Egyptians, are at the heart of modern civilization and culture. Instead of wandering to and fro, grinding wild oats and plant roots and spreading old porridge on hot rocks, humans began to stay in one place, farming and harvesting wheat and baking leavened breads in ovens. While they did this, they also built cities and created governments and more organized versions of civilizations. Furthermore, now every single person didn't have to spend their time acquiring food. They began to paint pictures, write stories and plays, and create myths, religions, and philosophies. Everything that was written down or rendered in art made it possible to share ideas and make progress.

# Naan

Making Indian naan is simple and similar to making pita. It contains yogurt, a product of milk and fermentation made originally in India. The traditional way to make this flatbread is to slap it on a hot wall inside fire-heated ovens called tandoors. These ovens are still in use today, but you can make your naan at home using a large skillet with a lid.

*Makes 4 naan*

| INGREDIENT | WEIGHT | VOLUME |
|---|---|---|
| All-purpose flour | 200 g | 1⅔ cups |
| Whole wheat flour | 100 g | ¾ cup plus 2 tablespoons |
| Water | 100 g | ¼ cup plus 3 tablespoons |
| Plain yogurt (not Greek-style) | 90 g | ⅓ rounded cup |
| Canola oil or other neutral oil | 10 g | 1½ teaspoons, plus more for the pan |
| Instant yeast | 4 g | ½ rounded teaspoon |
| Fine salt | 6 g | 1 teaspoon |

**Prepare:** Weigh or measure the ingredients and gather your supplies.

**Mix:** In a large bowl, combine both flours with the water, yogurt, oil, yeast, and salt. Mix by hand, using a grab-and-squish motion to thoroughly combine all the ingredients, until the dough comes together in a smooth ball.

**Knead:** Turn the dough out onto a lightly floured work surface. Knead the dough with a push-and-fold motion. Firmly push the dough away from you, then fold it back toward you, rotating the dough a quarter turn every few folds. Repeat pushing and folding for about 5 minutes, or until the dough is smooth and not sticky or tacky.

**Rise:** Return the dough to the bowl, cover it with a kitchen towel (or plastic wrap, if necessary, in drier climates), and let rise in a warm place for 60 minutes. It will puff slightly, but this is a flatbread so the dough will not rise significantly.

**Divide and Shape:** Turn the risen dough out onto a lightly floured work surface. Divide the dough into 4 pieces, roughly 120 grams each. Use your hands to gently round each piece into a ball, then place them on your work surface. Cover the balls with a kitchen towel and let them rest for 20 minutes.

To make naan, stretch each dough ball gently by hand like you would stretch a pizza, aiming for a triangular shape with rounded edges, about 5 by 7 inches (13 by 18 cm).

continued

**naan, continued**

## old bread and its many forms

The question of what to do with day-old bread has been on the minds of people all over the world for centuries. It seems the most popular solution wherever you are is a combination of oil and heat. In the case of tortillas and pita, there's tortilla and pita chips, and with bread we have toast or croutons. (You can easily make your own tortillas or pitas into chips by coating them in oil and baking. Use the recipe for croutons on page 92 as a guideline—it's the same idea.) Even leftover rice is often turned into fried rice with the application of oil and heat. What other foods can you think of that get repurposed this way? Do you make anything like this at home?

**Cook:** Just like with the pita, we will cook these in a skillet with a lid. Heat a large skillet with a glass lid over medium-high heat and lightly grease the pan with oil.

Place a stretched naan in the heated pan and cover with the lid. After 45 to 60 seconds, little bubbles will dot the surface of the dough.

Remove the lid, flip the bubbly naan with tongs or a spatula, and cook on the other side for about a minute longer. When you flip it, it should have some beautiful brown scorch marks and be visibly puffed in random areas. You may have to reduce the heat as you cook each subsequent naan, as the pan may retain heat. Be mindful and alert!

To enjoy, eat plain or brush with some garlic butter (recipe follows).

These are best when eaten the same day but can be stored in a resealable plastic bag for up to 3 days.

# Garlic Butter

Making a compound butter (butter with herbs and flavorings) is a simple technique that can add tons of flavor to all kinds of dishes. Make this garlic butter to brush onto warm naan or to make garlic bread with other bread recipes. You can get creative and add other herbs and spices to make different kinds of butters.

Makes ½ cup (140 g)

| INGREDIENT | WEIGHT | VOLUME |
|---|---|---|
| Salted butter, at room temperature | 113 g | 1 stick (½ cup) |
| Garlic, chopped | | 3 cloves |
| Fresh flat-leaf parsley or cilantro, roughly chopped | 15 g | ¼ cup |

In a small saucepan over low heat, warm the butter and garlic, stirring gently, just until the garlic becomes fragrant and lightly toasted. Be careful not to burn the butter or garlic. Pour the warm butter into a bowl and scatter in the chopped herbs. Brush this over naan for a delicious garlic naan.

To store, pour the butter into an airtight container and cover it. It will become solid again and you can store it in the fridge for up to one week. You can also mold it into a log and store it in waxed paper in the fridge.

# Lentil Cakes

In biblical times, during famines, simple breads were said to have been made with barley, millet, or spelt. When wheat became scarce, many people tried to make bread out of other grains and legumes. There aren't many commercially available breads today made with legumes, but there is a popular thin pancake made from lentils and millet or rice in India called dosa; Italians make a thick pancake of ground chickpeas called socca or farinata; in France crepes are made from the pseudo-grain buckwheat; and Ethiopians make a pancake of teff called injera. These lentil cakes are quick and easy to make, high in protein, and satisfying to eat.

*Makes about 4 cakes*

| INGREDIENT | WEIGHT | VOLUME |
|---|---|---|
| Dry red lentils | 150 g | about ¾ cup |
| All-purpose flour | 150 g | 1¼ cups |
| Water | 320 g | 1⅓ cups |
| Fine salt | 4 g | ½ rounded teaspoon |
| Neutral oil, for the pan | | |

Lentil cakes will cook just like a pancake does. When you see bubbles start to form and pop on the surface, it's time to flip the cake.

**Prepare:** Weigh or measure all the ingredients and gather your supplies.

In a large bowl filled with water, wash the lentils thoroughly by swirling them with your hands, then pour off the water. Cover the lentils with water again and let them soak for 1 hour.

**Mix:** In a blender or food processor, combine the drained lentils, flour, water, and salt and blend until completely smooth. The batter should have the consistency of heavy cream or thin pancake batter.

**Cook:** Heat a large skillet over medium-high heat and lightly grease the pan with oil. Pour about 1 cup of batter into the skillet and cook for 1 minute, or until you see bubbles pop all over the surface. Flip the cake with a spatula and cook on the other side for about a minute longer. There should be a bubble pattern on the surface and some browning. Repeat with all the batter.

Lentil cakes are best when eaten while still warm. Enjoy them plain or spread with salted butter or soft cheese.

# Apple Cider Barm Bread

Barm is a yeast derived from the beer-making process. Since beer (from wheat), mead (from honey), and cider (from apples and other fruits) are all produced by wild yeast fermentation, just like bread, the brewer and baker typically had a close symbiotic relationship during medieval times. Cider grew in popularity in the 13th century, when there was a need for clean liquids to drink. By the 15th century, medieval folks were using cider as a form of currency, and it was so popular it was responsible for the domestication and aggressive propagation of apples. We'll make this bread with nonalcoholic apple cider—Martinelli's is a great choice. The gentle aroma of the sweet apples is beautiful in this bread, and it is great to eat with a hearty soup in the fall or winter.          Makes 1 loaf

| INGREDIENT | WEIGHT | VOLUME |
| --- | --- | --- |
| All-purpose flour | 400 g | 3⅓ cups |
| Whole wheat flour | 100 g | ¾ cup plus 2 tablespoons |
| Nonalcoholic apple cider | 330 g | 1⅓ cups |
| Molasses | 20 g | 1 tablespoon |
| Instant yeast | 10 g | 1 rounded tablespoon |
| Fine salt | 10 g | 1½ teaspoons |

**Prepare:** Weigh or measure all the ingredients and gather your supplies. Bring the cider to the correct temperature, using the temperature chart (see page 27).

**Mix:** In a large bowl, combine both flours with the cider, molasses, yeast, and salt. Mix by hand, using a grab-and-squish motion to thoroughly combine all the ingredients, until the dough is smooth and there are no dry bits of flour.

**Rest:** Cover the bowl with a kitchen towel and let the dough rest for 20 minutes.

**Knead:** Turn the dough out onto a lightly floured work surface. Knead the dough with a push-and-fold motion. Firmly push the dough away from you, then fold it back toward you, rotating the dough a quarter turn every few folds. Repeat pushing and folding for about 5 minutes, or until the dough is smooth and not sticky or tacky.

**Rise:** Return the dough to the bowl, cover with a kitchen towel (or plastic wrap, if necessary, in drier climates), and let it rise for 60 minutes.

**Shape:** This bread is shaped into a round loaf and baked free form, the way it might have been baked on a hearth long ago. Turn the dough out onto a lightly floured work surface, with the smooth top of the dough face down, leaving the underside facing up. Gently pat the dough out into a rough square shape. Fold the farthest edge of the dough in toward you, tacking it down in the middle of the dough. Then fold the near edge up to meet it in the middle, essentially performing a letter fold. Now turn the dough a quarter turn, and fold those edges the same way. You will end with a somewhat squared-off parcel. Turn this over and gently round the dough into a ball with your hands.

**Proof:** Place a kitchen towel in a large clean bowl, basket, or colander and dust it well with flour. Place the loaf with the seam side down in the towel. This will allow the loaf to retain the round shape as it rises. Let the dough proof at room temperature for 45 minutes before baking.

**Make a Steam Chamber:** Fill a sturdy metal tray or metal roasting pan (no ceramic or glass, please) halfway with water and place the pan on the lowest shelf of your oven. This will create steam as the oven preheats.

**Preheat:** Preheat the oven to 450°F (230°C). If you have a pizza stone, you can preheat that along with the oven. If you don't have one, you can use a baking sheet.

**Bake:** Unmold your loaf from its resting place onto a sheet of parchment paper. Slide the loaf and the parchment paper onto the preheated pizza stone or baking sheet using a cutting board or pizza peel. Bake for 20 minutes, then open the oven to check on the loaf and let out the steam.

continued

**apple cider barm bread, continued**

Additional sugars in the dough from the cider will contribute to browning in the crust, and this loaf will have a beautiful color.

Be cautious of the escaping steam and keep your face away from the door. Your loaf will have opened and split apart along the seam and should be a pale golden color. Bake for 15 minutes longer, or until it is your desired shade of brown. I like a deep russet color on a loaf like this, like you would get in a hearth oven.

**Cool:** Transfer the bread to a wire rack and let cool for about 25 minutes. Enjoy with a hearty peasant stew—the flavor of the apple cider will be wonderful with it.

This bread is best when eaten the same day it is made.

## celtics and pagan love for bread

Barm bread survived with the Celtic peoples in England, Scotland, and Ireland. Before Christianity spread from the Middle East and Rome to the northeast of Europe, that region practiced paganism, a nature-based religion whose adherents worshipped many gods related to the harvest. For example, John Barleycorn, the "living spirit of the grain," dies so bread can be produced—Barleycorn is reborn as the seed returns to the earth. Death and rebirth is a common theme in all religions, codified with the practices for growing grain and harvesting grain. Lammas is the pagan celebration of the grain harvest, a time for gathering and giving thanks for abundance.

To celebrate Lammas (also called "Loaf Mass"), a loaf of bread was baked and blessed to protect the harvest. Lammas is a time of transformation, rebirth, and new beginnings. Taking care of one's crops once meant the difference between life and death, hence the dominance of grain in many cultures and religions, rituals, and daily prayers.

# Fresh Butter

It's great fun to make butter, and it's incredible how simple it is, especially if you have someone to take turns shaking it with you. The shaking jar replicates an old-fashioned butter churn, which agitates the cream, eventually separating the butter solids from the liquid to make butter—and buttermilk!

Makes about 1 cup (600 g) butter and 1 cup (300 g) buttermilk

| INGREDIENT | WEIGHT | VOLUME |
|---|---|---|
| Heavy whipping cream, at room temperature | 908 g | 2 cups |
| Flaky sea salt, to finish | | |

Pour the cream into a large 4-cup (32-ounce) mason jar and screw the lid on tightly. Shake the jar vigorously for 3 to 5 minutes (taking turns if you can). The cream will thicken at first and then start to separate into chunks—keep going and it will start to form into a ball, with some liquid left over. At this point, pour the contents of the jar into a strainer over a bowl. In the strainer you will have butter and in the bowl you will have buttermilk, which you can use to make pancakes.

Spread some butter on a slice of bread, then sprinkle flaky sea salt over the top. Butter can be stored in the fridge wrapped in waxed paper for a week or two.

apple cider barm bread, page 164

fresh butter, page 167

# Rye, Wheat, and Corn Bread

Before wheat was fully established in North America, Pilgrims and their descendants ate brown bread. This "thirded" bread was originally made from equal parts of three grains: rye, which was brought to the New World by Europeans; corn, which was native to the Americas; and wheat, which was on the rise in North America. This recipe is a loose approximation made with mostly wheat flour so that you can taste the three flavors of flours. You can use a loaf pan to bake it, but feel free to experiment with a greased clay flowerpot or a coffee can, which is how it was made in colonial times.    Makes 1 loaf

| INGREDIENT | WEIGHT | VOLUME |
|---|---|---|
| Water | 340 g | 1¼ cups plus 3 tablespoons |
| Canola oil or other neutral oil | 30 g | 2 tablespoons |
| Molasses | 25 g | 1 rounded tablespoon |
| Instant yeast | 10 g | 1 rounded tablespoon |
| All-purpose flour | 500 g | 4 cups |
| Rye flour | 50 g | ½ cup |
| Masa harina | 50 g | ¼ cup plus 3 tablespoons |
| Fine salt | 14 g | 2½ teaspoons |

**Prepare:** Weigh or measure all the ingredients and gather your supplies. Bring the water to the correct temperature, using the temperature chart (see page 27).

**Mix:** In a large bowl, combine the water, oil, molasses, and yeast and whisk well. Add the all-purpose and rye flours, masa harina, and salt. Mix by hand, using a grab-and-squish motion to thoroughly combine all the ingredients. The dough is well mixed when it is smooth and there are no dry bits of flour. This may take about 5 minutes.

Rye and corn don't have much of the protein that forms gluten, so the texture of this dough will feel different to you (100 percent rye bread doughs have a texture similar to mud). Don't worry when this dough is a bit dense and produces a cornbread or cakelike texture.

**Rest:** Cover the bowl with a kitchen towel and let the dough rest for 20 minutes.

**Knead:** Turn the dough out onto a well-floured work surface. Knead the dough with a push-and-fold motion. Firmly push the dough away from you, then fold it back toward you, rotating the dough a quarter turn every few folds. Repeat pushing and folding for about 5 minutes, or until the dough feels smooth, tight, and bouncy. Don't let the dough stick to your hands or the work surface; dust with more flour as needed.

continued

**Rise:** Return the dough to the bowl, cover it with a kitchen towel (or plastic wrap, if necessary, in drier climates), and let rise for 90 minutes. The dough should increase in size by roughly half.

**Shape:** Turn the dough out onto a lightly floured work surface. Gently pat the dough out into a rough rectangle shape (10 by 15 inches/23 by 38 cm). Fold in the corners farthest from you as if you were folding in the sleeves of a T-shirt, then roll the dough up toward you like a yoga mat. Place it in a 9 by 5-inch (23 by 13 by 6 cm) loaf pan with the seam side down.

**Proof:** Let the loaf proof, uncovered, at room temperature in the loaf pan for 45 minutes to an hour. A fully proofed loaf should rise above the edges of the pan and leave a soft impression when you press on it.

**Preheat:** While the loaf is proofing, preheat the oven to 425°F (220°C).

**Bake:** Bake for 28 to 32 minutes, until the top has a deep brown color. Peek halfway through the bake time and rotate the pan for a more even bake. Unmold the loaf from the pan right away and transfer to a wire rack to let cool for about 30 minutes. Enjoy with butter.

The rye and molasses will give this bread an excellent freshness; store it in a paper bag for 3 or 4 days.

# Potato Bread

It did not take potato growers long to find a way to make flour from potatoes. However, potato flour is not enough to make bread because it does not develop gluten, which gives bread its shape. In Germany, potato bread may contain spelt and rye flour, while in Scotland, tattie scones are made from mashed potatoes and just enough flour to make a dough that can be rolled and cut. In Ireland, there's pratie oaten, made with mashed potatoes and rolled oats, while Nordic countries enjoy lefse, a delicate potato-based crepe. Here, the texture of the mashed potato helps make this bread wonderfully soft.

Makes 1 loaf

| INGREDIENT | WEIGHT | VOLUME |
|---|---|---|
| Water | 280 g | 1 cup plus 2 tablespoons |
| Russet potatoes (or any other variety you prefer), peeled, boiled, and mashed | 150 g | ¾ cup, from 2 to 3 potatoes |
| Instant yeast | 10 g | 1 rounded tablespoon |
| All-purpose flour | 400 g | 3½ cups |
| Whole wheat flour | 100 g | ¾ cup plus 2 tablespoons |
| Honey (or any liquid sweetener you like) | 10 g | 1 rounded teaspoon |
| Fine salt | 12 g | 2 teaspoons |

**Prepare:** Weigh or measure all the ingredients and gather your supplies. Bring the water to the correct temperature, using the temperature chart (see page 27). Let the mashed potatoes cool to room temperature.

**Mix:** In a large bowl, combine the water, mashed potatoes, and yeast. Use a spoon to mix gently until the yeast is dispersed. Add both flours, the honey, and the salt. Mix by hand, using a grab-and-squish motion to thoroughly combine all the ingredients. The dough is well mixed when it is smooth and there are no dry bits of flour. This may take about 5 minutes.

**Rest:** Cover the bowl with a kitchen towel and let the dough rest for 15 minutes.

**Knead:** Turn the dough out onto a well-floured work surface. Knead the dough with a push-and-fold motion. Firmly push the dough away from you, then fold it back toward you, rotating the dough a quarter turn every few folds. Repeat pushing and folding for about 5 minutes, or until the dough feels smooth, tight, and bouncy. Don't let the dough stick to your hands or the work surface; dust with more flour as needed.

continued

## potato bread, continued

Potatoes have natural sugars inside them that yeasts really like! This dough might rise more quickly because of the potatoes in the dough, so keep an eye on this one.

$\rightarrow$

**Rise:** Return the dough to the bowl, cover it with a kitchen towel (or plastic wrap, if necessary, in drier climates), and let rise for 90 minutes. The dough should increase in size by roughly half.

**Shape:** Turn the dough out onto a lightly floured work surface. Gently pat the dough out into a rough rectangle shape (about 8 by 12 inches/20 by 27 cm). Fold in the corners farthest from you as if you were folding in the sleeves of a T-shirt, then roll the dough up toward you like a yoga mat. Place it in a 9 by 5-inch (23 by 13 by 6 cm) loaf pan with the seam side down.

**Proof:** Let the loaf proof, uncovered, at room temperature in the loaf pan for 45 minutes to an hour. A fully proofed loaf should rise above the edges of the pan and leave a soft impression when you press on it.

**Preheat:** While the loaf is proofing, preheat the oven to 425°F (220°C).

**Bake:** Bake for 28 to 32 minutes, until the top has a pale golden color. Peek halfway through the bake time and rotate the pan for a more even bake. Unmold the loaf from the pan right away and transfer to a wire rack to let cool for 30 minutes.

The potato in this loaf gives it great freshness for about 3 days. Store it in a resealable plastic bag to keep it soft.

### starches as staple foods in different cultures

Grains—wheat, oats, rice, corn—and the products made from them have become staple foods that feed the world. Throughout history we've seen these grains occasionally become scarce due to droughts or famine, and people turn to other starches to keep them full. These include potatoes, lentils, cassava, plantains, soybeans, and more. Ask your children, What kinds of starches do you most commonly eat besides grains? What about your classmates or friends? How much of your daily meals are made up of wheat, oats, rice, or corn, and what would you replace them with if you couldn't eat grains for a day?

# Brioche

Brioche originated in France possibly as early as the 1400s but really became popular in the 17th century. With a flour-to-butter ratio that is sometimes as high as 2:1, brioche was also historically enriched with eggs, milk, and sugar and produced from sifted white flour, which made for a wildly expensive loaf at the time. This brioche recipe has less butter in it, which makes it a bit easier to mix by hand, but it is still a special-occasion bread and a delight to eat.

*Makes 1 loaf*

| INGREDIENT | WEIGHT | VOLUME |
|---|---|---|
| Whole milk | 200 g | ¾ cup plus 2 tablespoons |
| Large eggs | | 2 |
| Unsalted butter, at room temperature | 100 g | 4 tablespoons |
| Sugar | 30 g | 2 tablespoons plus 1½ teaspoons |
| Instant yeast | 10 g | 1 rounded tablespoon |
| All-purpose flour | 400 g | 3½ cups |
| Fine salt | 8 g | 1 rounded teaspoon |

**Prepare:** Weigh or measure all the ingredients and gather your supplies. Bring the milk to the correct temperature, using the temperature chart (see page 27).

**Mix:** In a large bowl, combine the milk, eggs, butter, sugar, and yeast. Use a spoon to mix gently until the yeast is dispersed. Add the flour and salt. Mix by hand, using a grab-and-squish motion to thoroughly combine all the ingredients. The dough is well mixed when it is smooth and there are no dry bits of flour. This may take about 5 minutes.

**Rest:** Cover the bowl with a kitchen towel and let the dough rest for 15 minutes.

**Knead:** Turn the dough out onto a well-floured work surface. Knead the dough with a push-and-fold motion. Firmly push the dough away from you, then fold it back toward you, rotating the dough a quarter turn every few folds. Repeat pushing and folding for about 5 minutes, or until the dough feels smooth, tight, and bouncy. Don't let the dough stick to your hands or the work surface; dust with more flour as needed.

**Rise:** Return the dough to the bowl, cover it with a kitchen towel (or plastic wrap, if necessary, in drier climates), and let rise for 90 minutes. The dough should increase in size by roughly half.

This traditional loaf is called brioche Nanterre, whose shape allows the soft bread to rise beautifully. Its light, feathery texture is revealed when you pull it apart.

If the dough gets cold, the butter will solidify inside the dough and make it very difficult to get a good rise, so try to keep this dough in a warm area while proofing.

**Divide and Shape:** Turn the risen dough out onto a lightly floured work surface. Gently pat into a rectangle shape. Divide the dough into 8 pieces, roughly 100 grams each. Use your hands to round each piece into a ball, then place the balls in a 9 by 5-inch (23 by 13 by 6 cm) loaf pan, lining them up in two rows lengthwise. They will rise together and create a loaf with 8 bumps on top.

**Proof:** Let the loaf proof, uncovered, in a warm area in the pan for 1½ to 2 hours. A fully proofed loaf should rise above the edges of the pan and leave a soft impression when you press on it; it will have a bumpy top.

**Preheat:** While the loaf is proofing, preheat the oven to 425°F (220°C).

**Bake:** Bake for 28 to 32 minutes, until the top has a golden color. Peek halfway through the bake time and rotate the pan for a more even bake. Unmold the loaf from the pan right away and transfer to a wire rack to let cool for 30 minutes.

The bread stays fresh for about 3 days. Slice it before storing in a resealable plastic bag to keep it soft. Use it for toast and sandwiches—or its best possible purpose, French toast!

## let them eat cake!

Though originating in France, brioche has traveled and migrated to other cultures. Italians enjoy panettone, a beautiful enriched bread made at Christmastime, while Spaniards and Mexicans eat pan dulce. The Portuguese brought pao doce to Hawaii, where you will often find Hawaiian sweet rolls, too, and when it migrated from there to Japan, it became shokupan, a sweet milk bread.

No enriched dough will ever be quite as historically significant or notorious as the French brioche, though. In the late 1700s, grains were in short supply during a period of economic struggle in France. In 1789, Queen Marie Antoinette is said to have advised, regarding peasants who had no bread, *"Qu'ils mangent de la brioche,"* commonly translated as "Let them eat cake," but she was really saying "Let them eat brioche." This flippant statement is said to have factored into the rise of the French Revolution and the execution of the queen and King Louis XVI.

brioche, page 176

# Wonder Bread

Industrialization led to a whiter loaf of bread than had ever been made before. Unfortunate side effects of this advancement, which began around the 1860s, included consumers suffering from malnutrition. Stripping the bran away from the flour and bleaching to create a soft white-flour bread also stripped away the nutrients and vitamins. Wonder Bread was one of the first enriched breads to contain added vitamins to prevent malnutrition. These added nutrients, the bread's fluffy and supersoft texture, and its convenience (presliced!) helped it become the bestselling bread in North America. Aggressive television advertising sealed the deal, and Wonder Bread became a household name. Make a classic PB&J or grilled cheese on this fluffy and sweet white bread, and maybe take a multivitamin, too.

*Makes 1 loaf*

| INGREDIENT | WEIGHT | VOLUME |
|---|---|---|
| Whole milk | 200 g | ¾ cup plus 2 tablespoons |
| Canola oil or other neutral oil | 100 g | ½ cup |
| Sugar | 30 g | 2 tablespoons plus 1½ teaspoons |
| Instant yeast | 10 g | 1 rounded tablespoon |
| All-purpose flour | 400 g | 3⅓ cups |
| Fine salt | 8 g | 1 rounded teaspoon |

**Prepare:** Weigh or measure all the ingredients and and gather your supplies. Bring the milk to the correct temperature, using the temperature chart (see page 27).

**Mix:** In a large bowl, combine the milk, oil, sugar, and yeast. Use a spoon to mix gently until the yeast is dispersed. Add the flour and salt. Mix by hand, using a grab-and-squish motion to thoroughly combine all the ingredients. The dough is well mixed when it is smooth and there are no dry bits of flour. This may take about 5 minutes.

**Rest:** Cover the bowl with a kitchen towel and let the dough rest for 15 minutes.

**Knead:** Turn the dough out onto a well-floured work surface. Knead the dough with a push-and-fold motion. Firmly push the dough away from you, then fold it back toward you, rotating the dough a quarter turn every few folds. Repeat pushing and folding for about 5 minutes, or until the dough feels smooth, tight, and bouncy. Don't let the dough stick to your hands or the work surface; dust with more flour as needed.

*continued*

## make your own bread crumbs

White bread made without preservatives tends to go stale quickly, but one great use for stale bread is making bread crumbs. This not only uses up old bread but avoids food waste, too.

All you need are a few slices of bread that have gone dry. If the bread is not completely dry, place the slices on a sheet pan and bake in a 400°F (200°C) oven for 15 minutes or so. Pulse the dried bread in a food processor or blender until it is fine textured, like sand.

Store your homemade bread crumbs in a dry airtight container. Use them to sprinkle on top of pasta or macaroni and cheese.

**Rise:** Return the dough to the bowl, cover it with a kitchen towel (or plastic wrap, if necessary, in drier climates), and let rise for 90 minutes. The dough should increase in size by roughly half.

**Shape:** Turn the risen dough out onto a lightly floured work surface. Gently pat the dough out into a rough rectangle shape (about 10 by 15 inches/25 by 38 cm). Fold in the corners farthest from you as if you were folding in the sleeves of a T-shirt, then roll the dough up toward you like a yoga mat. Place the dough in a 9 by 5-inch (23 by 13 by 6 cm) loaf pan with the seam side down.

**Proof:** Let the loaf proof, uncovered, at room temperature in the loaf pan for 45 minutes to an hour. A fully proofed loaf should rise above the edges of the pan and leave a soft impression when you press on it.

**Preheat:** While the loaf is proofing, preheat the oven to 425°F (220°C).

**Bake:** Bake for 28 to 32 minutes, until the top has a golden color. Peek halfway through the bake time and rotate the pan for a more even bake. Unmold the loaf from the pan right away and transfer to a wire rack to let cool for 30 minutes.

This loaf won't keep very long. Slice it and store it in a resealable plastic bag for 2 days. Use it to make a classic American sandwiches, and when it goes stale, make bread crumbs (see sidebar).

## whole-grain innovations and the american revolution

In the 1800s, Reverend Sylvester Graham claimed (correctly, as it turns out) that many beneficial nutrients were lost in the quest to create whiter, lighter bread. Though white breads were a status symbol at the time (only the poor ate brown whole-grain breads), Graham promoted bread made from unsifted, unbleached flour. Graham crackers are named after him and are still a household name, although the commercial product is not the same as what he envisioned.

Physician John Harvey Kellogg, a follower of Graham, believed in the same whole-grain diet and started making bran flakes, but the cereal that would make Kellogg famous ended up being a much sweeter version of his original bran flakes. The ever-popular Kellogg's Raisin Bran and Corn Flakes bear his name to this day.

Fiber-packed cereals and crackers soon became commercialized and industrialized and sweetened quite a bit in the process. Now wheat and whole-grain breads have overtaken Wonder Bread as bestsellers in the bread landscape. What will the next revolution be? Will handcrafted breads made with locally grown grains by home bakers and small local bakeries overtake commercially produced breads? That is a dream shared by the new generation of farmers, millers, and bakers taking their place in the long line of history. To read more about that, check out *The New Bread Basket* by Amy Halloran. You will be inspired.

# Whole-Grain Sandwich Loaf

Thanks to widespread interest in whole foods and whole-grain nutrition, a good whole-grain loaf is now seen as superior to a plain white loaf. Biodiversity in grain farming, small wheat farms growing heirloom varieties of grain, local millers, smaller artisan bakeries . . . all of these have grown in popularity over the past several decades, and it is now more common to find an artisanal baker in your community working with freshly milled local and heirloom whole grains. This bread is an approachable weekly loaf for toasts and sandwiches, with all the fiber and nutrients of the grain intact. The honey and oil give it a softness and sweetness to last through the week.

Makes 1 loaf

| INGREDIENT | WEIGHT | VOLUME |
|---|---|---|
| Water | 410 g | 1¾ cups |
| Canola oil or other neutral oil | 40 g | 3 tablespoons |
| Honey (or any liquid sweetener you like) | 40 g | 2 tablespoons |
| Instant yeast | 10 g | 1 rounded tablespoon |
| Whole wheat flour | 500 g | 4¼ cups |
| Fine salt | 12 g | 2 teaspoons |

Resting the dough gives the flour some time to absorb the liquid in the dough and relax.

**Prepare:** Weigh or measure all the ingredients and gather your supplies. Bring the water to the correct temperature, using the temperature chart (see page 27).

**Mix:** In a large bowl, combine the water, oil, honey, and yeast. Mix gently by hand until the yeast is dispersed. Add the flour and salt. Mix by hand, using a grab-and-squish motion to thoroughly combine all the ingredients. The dough is well mixed when it is smooth and there are no dry bits of flour. This may take about 5 minutes.

**Rest:** Cover the bowl with a kitchen towel and let the dough rest for 15 minutes.

**Knead:** Turn the dough out of the bowl onto a well-floured work surface. Knead the dough with a push-and-fold motion. Firmly push the dough away from you, then fold it back toward you, rotating the dough a quarter turn every few folds. Repeat pushing and folding for about 5 minutes, or until the dough feels smooth, tight, and bouncy. Don't let the dough stick to your hands or the work surface; dust with more flour as needed.

**Rise:** Return the dough to the bowl, cover it with a kitchen towel (or plastic wrap, if necessary, in drier climates), and let rise for 90 minutes. The dough should increase in size by roughly half.

continued

## whole-grain sandwich loaf, continued

When you place the dough in the loaf pan, make sure the seam side is down. That way when bread bakes, it will have a smooth surface across the top of the loaf.

**Shape:** Turn the dough out onto a lightly floured work surface. Gently pat the dough into a rough rectangle shape (about 10 by 15 inches/25 by 38 cm). Fold in the corners farthest from you as if you were folding in the sleeves of a T-shirt, then roll the dough up toward you like a yoga mat. Place it in a 9 by 5-inch (23 by 13 by 6 cm) loaf pan with the seam side down.

**Proof:** Let the loaf proof, uncovered, at room temperature in the loaf pan for 45 minutes to an hour. A fully proofed loaf should rise above the edges of the pan and leave a soft impression when you press on it.

**Preheat:** While the loaf is proofing, preheat the oven to 425°F (220°C).

**Bake:** Bake for 28 to 32 minutes, until the honey in the dough gives the top a beautiful golden color. Peek halfway through the bake time and rotate the pan for a more even bake. Unmold the loaf from the pan right away and transfer to a wire rack to let cool for 30 minutes.

This bread stays fresh for about 3 days. Slice it and store it in a resealable plastic bag to keep it soft.

# Sourdough Breads

RECIPES BASED IN MATH AND SCIENCE,
FOR AGES 12 AND UP

## In This Chapter

**You will practice . . .**

* **Using math to manipulate sourdough recipes**

* **Maintaining a sourdough starter**

* **Baking with whole grains**

* **Scoring bread**

Sourdough breads are leavened naturally by a homegrown culture of yeasts and bacteria. This baking style is typically considered the holy grail for serious bread bakers, yielding breads with nuanced flavor profiles, craft quality, and improved digestibility and nutrition. As a bonus, once you know how to make sourdough starter, you'll never need to buy commercial yeast packets again!

To understand what makes this style of bread unique, you'll want to start by diving into the math and science that are the engine of sourdough bread formulas (pages 194–195). Once you have a working overview of baker's percentages and sourdough starter cultivation, you can bake loaves that incorporate more whole grains and better nutrition. Try an Oatmeal or Multigrain Sourdough (page 214) and even a Sprouted Quinoa and Chia Sourdough (page 219). Making sourdough bread is advanced baking, but the result is worth the effort.

# Learning Opportunities

Making sourdough breads utilizes many of the same math and science skills that high school students typically focus on. Connecting those lessons to the bread they eat every day makes the concepts more tangible. With these recipes, you can take a supporting role and let your teen find the conclusions on their own while they practice the following concepts.

## Math

When broken down, recipes are a combination of numbers, processes, and variables. "Baker's percentages" is a mathematical method widely used in bread baking to calculate the amounts of ingredients. Sourdough recipes use percentages, multiplication, process order, averaging, multiplying, and dividing.

## Scientific Method

From forming a hypothesis to running an experiment, drawing conclusions, and manipulating variables, the scientific method is key to baking. Start by following a recipe step-by-step, and as you become more comfortable with the recipe's procedures, you can begin to riff on the original recipe, wondering, "What if?" What if I used less water in this dough? What if I used a different type of flour? The "what ifs" are the beginning of experimentation.

## Biology/Chemistry

The building blocks of sourdough bread include microbes, chemical compounds, proteins, enzymes, acids, and chemical transformations. Understanding these components and how they interact with each other makes for better bread bakers.

## Nutrition

Whole-grain bread provides fiber, minerals, and other nutrients. Inclusions like oats, seeds, and other grains can boost nutrition in our bread. Sourdough fermentation adds even more nutritional value. Learning how to make a nutrient-dense loaf of bread is a foundational skill for eating well for the rest of your life.

# Baker's Percentages and Mathematics

Baker's percentages, or baker's math, is a way of expressing a recipe's ingredients in relation to each other. Baker's percentage formulas are always expressed in weight, which allows for accuracy and easy scaling of recipes. We'll talk specifically about bread baking here, but any baking formula can be expressed this way.

In baker's math, the flour weight is always 100 percent, and the other ingredients are expressed as a percentage of that quantity of flour by weight. A lean dough, which is, as you'll recall, a dough made simply of flour, salt, yeast, and water (without any egg, butter, or oil), follows a specific and predictable pattern:

Salt is typically close to 2 percent of the flour by weight. It might be adjusted down to 1.8 percent (perhaps if other salty ingredients, like olives or cheese, are being added to the dough) or up to 2.2 percent (if you are including ingredients that need salt, like oats or more whole grains).

Yeast can vary based on the length of fermentation time desired, but usually it's around 1 percent of the flour weight. Less yeast will usually mean a longer fermentation time, while more yeast will create a more rapid rise. For sourdough recipes, the sourdough starter typically falls somewhere between 20 and 30 percent of the flour weight.

Water quantity, sometimes called "hydration," has a much wider range than the salt or yeast. Typically, hydration percentages are in the 60s and 70s, but when more whole grain is added to a dough, it's not uncommon to see those percentages up in the 80s and 90s.

Consider this sample dough recipe:

**Flour: 500 grams**

**Water: 340 grams**

**Salt: 10 grams**

**Yeast: 5 grams**

Now, to find the baker's percentages, convert each ingredient's weight into a percentage. Remember: The flour will always be 100 percent.

**Flour: 500 grams = 100%**

**Water: 340 ÷ 500 = 0.68 or 68%**

**Salt: 10 ÷ 500 = 0.02 or 2%**

**Yeast: 5 ÷ 500 = 0.01 or 1%**

**Total dough percentage: 100% + 68% + 2% × 1% = 171%**

You can see that all the ingredients in this sample recipe are in the predicted percentage range.

Now that we have the percentages, we can scale this recipe to any quantity. Let's say that you want to follow this recipe, but you want to use an entire 2,267-gram (5 pound) bag of flour at once. Simply multiply the percentages of each ingredient by the total quantity of flour. If you get decimals, just round up to the next gram.

| ORIGINAL RECIPE | SCALED-UP RECIPE (USING 2,267 GRAMS OF FLOUR) |
|---|---|
| Flour: 100% | Flour: 100 × 2,267 = 2,267 grams |
| Water: 68% | Water: 0.68 × 2,267 = 1,542 grams |
| Salt: 2% | Salt: 0.02 × 2,267 = 45 grams |
| Yeast: 1% | Yeast: 0.01 × 2,267 = 22 grams |
| Total dough: 171% | Total dough: 1.71 × 2,267 = 3,876 grams |

## pizza night math

Using the sample dough recipe (left), calculate the weight of the ingredients needed for the scenario below.

You're hosting a pizza night. You want to use 600 grams of dough for one pizza, and you're inviting 3 guests who will each make 1 pizza, so you'll need a total of 2,400 grams of dough.

Start by finding the conversion factor: Take your desired total dough weight of 2,400 grams (600 grams of dough for 4 people—don't forget yourself!) and divide it by the total dough percentage of the original recipe (171).

**2,400 ÷ 171 = 14**

Our conversion factor is 14. We'll multiply each ingredient percentage by 14 to get a new formula for making enough dough for 4 pizzas.

**Flour: 100 × 14 = 1,400 grams**

**Water: 68 × 14 = 952 grams**

**Salt: 2 × 14 = 28 grams**

**Yeast: 1 × 14 = 14 grams**

**Total dough: 2,394 grams**

Now let's tackle another scenario: Use the above formula to make enough pizza dough for your whole family. Each person will get a personal pizza made from a 300-gram dough ball. You can begin with the following calculation:

**300-gram dough ball × (the number of people in your family) = total dough required**

**total dough required ÷ 171 (the total dough percentage) = conversion factor**

# Temperature Calculations

Dough ferments best between 75° and 78°F (24° and 26°C). This target range is what bakers call the "desired dough temperature," or DDT. To control dough temperature, beginner bakers can note the ambient temperature of their baking environment and adjust their ingredient temperature according to the chart on page 27. But for improved accuracy, advanced bakers can do some simple math to achieve the perfect DDT. When you are making bread, there are a few factors that contribute to the overall temperature of the final dough. To begin, you have the air temperature of the room you are baking in, the temperature of the flour, and the temperature of the water used to mix the dough. Then you have the friction factor, which is the warmth you contribute through mixing and kneading; for doughs mixed by hand, this is usually around 5°F (3°C), while for a stand mixer it can be closer to a 20°F (11°C) increase.

The variable you can control to hit your DDT is the temperature of the water. To calculate the correct water temperature for your dough, multiply the desired dough temperature of 75°F (24°C) by the number of variables other than the water.

air + flour + friction = 3 variables

75 × 3 = 225

Then subtract the other factors from that total to find the target water temperature:

225 – air temperature – flour temperature – friction factor = target water temperature

Now that you understand the basic formula, you can account for additional variables, like working with a sourdough starter, which brings its own heat with it. Again, simply multiply your desired temperature by the total number of variables, which in this case is 4: air, flour, friction, and starter. Then subtract each variable from that total:

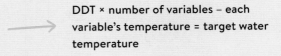

DDT × number of variables – each variable's temperature = target water temperature

This formula will allow you to produce consistent results regardless of the types of breads you make or the quantity of dough you need to produce.

## division for desired dough temperature

Here's an example formula to practice temperature calculations.

Let's say we're making a basic yeasted dough; our desired dough temperature (DDT) is 75°F (24°C). It was very cold last night and so it's 60°F (15°C) in our kitchen, the temperature of the flour is also 60°F (15°C), and we are mixing by hand.

To begin, multiply the DDT by the number of variables, which in this case is 3 (air temperature, flour temperature, and heat gain from friction):

75 × 3 = 225

Then subtract the actual value of those factors from that number:

225 – 60 (air temperature) – 60 (flour temperature) – 5 (friction factor mixing by hand) = 100

So, we will need water at 100°F (38°C) to reach our desired dough temperature in this cold house today.

Now it's your turn! Check the temperature in your house, and work out the calculations for a hand-mixed dough in your kitchen today.

# Proper Care and Feeding of Your Starter

Sourdoughs all over the world arise from harmonious combinations of yeasts and bacteria, the exact species and strains of which depend on the location and growing conditions. Your starter will be unique to you and your environment. Creating a starter requires consistency more than any other factor. Here are the best practices to make sure it thrives.

## TEMPERATURE

The starter should be kept in a warm spot, ideally where it's above 70°F (21°C). Try to find a neutral area that won't be subject to drastic temperature fluctuations. Starters subjected to frequent high temperatures can become rancid or sour, and the pH balance can be negatively affected. Avoid placing a starter near a sunny window in the summer, for example, or near a heat source such as an oven. Reliable temperature ranges ensure successful fermentation.

The other influence is the temperature of the water used for feeding the starter. Try to be consistent, using water between 75° and 80°F (24° and 27°C).

## WASTE REMOVAL

Before feeding a starter, remove and discard half of it as waste. A common error, especially among beginner sourdough bakers, is not removing half of the starter before feeding it. The starter needs to be refreshed with new food, and the waste products of acids and alcohols must be removed so the starter can maintain its pH and a balance of food for the yeasts and bacteria. Skipping the discard step will create an environment that the microbes cannot thrive in; the starter activity will become more sluggish and slower until the growth slows to

zero due to acidity. This is when you will notice strong alcohol and acetone aromas from the starter, or even a layer of liquid alcohol on the surface of the starter. Use a spoon to scoop half of the starter out of the jar and discard it. If you created your starter using the sourdough starter recipe (page 205), your starter should be about 60 grams and you want to discard enough so that only 30 grams remain. Discard can be stored in the fridge to use in other recipes or simply thrown away or composted. After discarding, it is time to feed the starter.

## 3

## FEEDING

It's a good practice to feed your starter at the same time each day, perhaps at a time when you are usually home. I like to feed my starter before bedtime and let it rise in the cooler temperatures during the night, so it will be ready for mixing in the morning. Someone who likes to bake in the afternoon when getting home from school or work should feed their starter in the morning when they wake up, so the yeast will have peaked by the time they arrive home.

It's important to be consistent while the culture is being established and not miss any feeding days. Once the starter is well established and the yeasts and bacteria are sturdier, a missed feeding here or there won't be a big deal.

Sourdough starters are always fed with equal parts flour and water (or at a ratio of 1:1). To feed the starter, place the jar of remaining starter on your scale. If you're creating a new starter according to the starter recipe (page 205) or you're feeding your starter between bakes, you should have about 30 grams of starter left after discarding, and then you'll follow the recipe on page 205 to feed it. To feed and scale your starter before a bake, look at the first step of your recipe's instructions to see how much flour and water you need to feed your starter to create enough starter to make that bread. Add the flour and water to the jar with the remaining starter and stir until it is well combined and no dry flour remains. This restarts the process, and a starter with healthy microbial activity will slowly expand and grow to its next peak. When it peaks, it is ready for baking again.

## LONG-TERM STORAGE AND CARE

Most home bakers don't bake every single day and will fall into a rhythm of working with a starter only once a week or so. To avoid having to feed the starter each day and waste flour, you can hold the starter in the fridge (remember: yeast rises slowly at cold temperatures), or you can used dried starter.

If you store your starter in the fridge, you can feed it just once a week. In this case, discard 90 percent of it instead of the usual half, then feed it according to the recipe on page 205.

Don't forget the weekly feeding! If a starter is stored for months without attention, it will develop an off-putting smell, a thick layer of alcohol at the top, and a dark gray/black color. Please don't let this happen to your hard-won starter! Store your starter in the front of the fridge so you don't forget about it.

Drying starter is less common, but it is one of my favorite methods for preservation. Dilute a portion of your starter with water until it has a thin consistency, like that of pancake batter. Use a spatula to spread a thin layer on parchment paper, then allow it to dry at room temperature (this will take about a day). The starter will dry into a thin sheet that can be crumbled into flakes. Put these dried flakes through a blender to reduce them to a powder. Store this dried starter in an airtight container at room temperature (don't forget to label it); it will keep indefinitely. When you want to reconstitute the starter, use a tablespoon of the powder as you would flour and follow the instructions for beginning a starter (see page 205). After a couple of feedings, you will have a fresh starter. I highly recommend keeping a dried starter as a backup for your refrigerated starter. It's also a great way to travel with or ship sourdough. You can put your powdered dried starter in an envelope or a resealable plastic bag for transport.

Making dried starter from your discard is a great way to repurpose it and share it with friends!

## put your sourdough discard to use

It's a bummer to waste flour, and there are many uses for sourdough starter discard. A starter that is at 100 percent hydration (or equal parts flour and water by weight) can be added to almost any baking project to give it a delicious, more complex flavor. You can keep discard in a jar in the fridge until you want to incorporate it into another recipe.

Start experimenting with sourdough discard by adding some to your pancake batter. The key, for any recipe, is that the starter discard portion stays at about 100 grams (scant ½ cup) or so, and that the recipe has another source of leavening, such as baking soda or baking powder, since the discard won't add much leavening power at this point. When the starter is an equal balance of water and flour and the addition of discard starter is kept small, it will enhance simple recipes without drastically changing them.

# Sourdough Starter

Sourdough starter is, at heart, a cultivated community of beneficial yeasts and bacteria that work together to leaven bread. These microbes grow exponentially when kept within an ideal environment and temperature range and replenished with "food" (flour and water) at a reliable rate, and with the removal of the "waste" (sometimes called discard) from the container to keep the culture medium in balance. Proper care ensures that the good organisms grow and outcompete any harmful bacteria.

It takes 5 to 7 days to create starter to be used for bread baking. Once you've created your starter, follow the instructions on page 198 for care, feeding, and storage to keep your starter alive between bakes. This recipe yields a small amount of starter that you can maintain between bakes without wasting large amounts of flour. Follow the first step of each recipe to scale your starter to the amount needed to make that bread.

| INGREDIENT | WEIGHT | VOLUME |
|---|---|---|
| Whole wheat flour | 15 g | 2 tablespoons |
| All-purpose flour | 15 g | 2 tablespoons |
| Filtered water | 30 g | 3 tablespoons |

Sourdough starters are fed with equal parts flour and water (or a ratio of 1:1). This means you can easily grow your starter by feeding it larger portions of flour and water, or you can maintain a small starter by feeding it little amounts of flour and water—so long as they remain in equal proportion.

**Mix:** In a large widemouthed mason jar, mix the whole wheat flour, all-purpose flour, and water. Cover the jar with a paper coffee filter, and secure with the metal ring that would normally hold the lid or a rubber band. The next day, or after 24 hours, remove 30 grams (3 tablespoons) of starter and feed the starter with the same combination of flour and water. Repeat this process for the next 6 days. Keep the jar at room temperature on your kitchen counter, where you will see it and remember to feed it.

One of the negative by-products of fermentation is alcohol. If you do not remove the waste matter from the starter daily, the fermentation process will continue to produce alcohol. Too much alcohol upsets the pH balance of the starter. If the alcohol proportion rises above 8 percent, it will slow or kill off the beneficial yeasts and bacteria. An easy way to gauge the health of your starter is to use your sense of smell. An established culture will have a sweet, almost fruity aroma, but it will go through a range of smells as it develops until it becomes established with the correct microbial mix.

Take notes in your baker's journal, noticing if any visible air bubbles have risen in the jar, indicating positive signs of fermentation. When it is properly established, the culture will double in size and smell like overripe fruit or yogurt.

# Simple Sourdough Tinned Loaf

The flavor payoff of making a sourdough loaf is absolutely worth the effort. The important thing to remember is that baking sourdough doesn't need to be intimidating; it's just adding one more variable to the ongoing experiment of breadmaking. It may take a bit of practice to capture the starter at its peak as it rises and falls. Remember that your starter may typically rise more slowly at night, during lower-temperature hours, than in the daytime. This is where the notes you take will come in handy; piece together the data you collect and use it to improve your baking.

*Makes 1 loaf*

| INGREDIENT | WEIGHT | VOLUME |
| --- | --- | --- |
| For the Starter: | | |
| All-purpose flour | 75 g | ½ cup plus 2 tablespoons |
| Water | 75 g | ¼ cup plus 1 tablespoon |
| For the Dough: | | |
| Water | 260 g | 1 cup plus 2 tablespoons |
| All-purpose flour | 300 g | 2½ cups |
| Whole wheat flour | 100 g | ¾ cup plus 2 tablespoons |
| Fine salt | 8 g | 1 rounded teaspoon |

**Feed and Scale the Starter:** Eight to 12 hours before mixing the dough, discard half of the starter (see page 198), then scale your starter to the amount needed in this recipe by feeding it with the amounts of flour and water indicated in the ingredients chart. Let the starter rise to its peak; it should double or triple in size in the container over the 8 to 12 hours.

Don't forget to feed your retained starter according to the feeding schedule in the initial sourdough starter formula!

**Prepare:** Weigh or measure all the ingredients and gather your supplies. Bring the water to the correct temperature, using the temperature chart (see page 27).

**Mix:** To make the dough, in a large bowl, combine the water and 120 grams (1 cup) of sourdough starter. Use a spoon to mix gently until the starter is dispersed. (Set aside the remaining portion of the starter in its original container to retain your starter.) Add both flours and the salt. Mix by hand, using a grab-and-squish motion to thoroughly combine all the ingredients. The dough is well mixed when it is smooth and there are no dry bits of flour. This may take about 5 minutes.

continued

# sourdough baking timelines

## Option 1

Friday, 9 p.m.: Refresh and feed the starter.

Saturday, 9 a.m.: Mix the dough with starter that has doubled in size.

Saturday, 9 a.m. to 12 p.m.: Let the dough rise.

Saturday, 1 p.m.: Shape and proof the dough.

Saturday, 1 p.m. to 2:30 p.m.: Bake and cool the bread.

## Option 2

Friday, 8 a.m.: Refresh and feed the starter.

Friday, 4 p.m. (or after work/school): Mix the dough with starter that has doubled in size.

Friday, 4 p.m. to 7 p.m.: Let the dough rise.

Friday, 8 p.m.: Shape and proof the dough.

Friday, after 8 p.m.: Put the loaf into the fridge and bake at leisure on Saturday morning.

**Rest:** Cover the bowl with a kitchen towel and let the dough rest for 15 minutes.

**Knead:** Turn the dough out onto a well-floured work surface. Knead the dough with a push-and-fold motion. Firmly push the dough away from you, then fold it back toward you, rotating the dough a quarter turn every few folds. Repeat pushing and folding for about 5 minutes, or until the dough feels smooth, tight, and bouncy. Don't let the dough stick to your hands or the work surface; dust with more flour as needed.

Remember that sourdough fermentation moves at a slightly slower pace than that of yeasted breads. Look for the small signs of fermentation like the appearance of small bubbles on the surface of the resting dough. Sometimes the first few bakes with a new starter can have a sluggish rise while the young starter stabilizes. Practicing and learning from each experiment is the goal.

**Rise:** Return the dough to the bowl, cover it with a kitchen towel (or plastic wrap, if necessary, in drier climates), and let rise for 2 to 3 hours. The dough should increase in size by roughly half. Leavened sourdough naturally rises at a slightly slower pace than yeasted doughs. You'll know the yeast is rising when the dough domes up slightly in the center and the surface has small bubbles all over it. Sourdough can be more sensitive to changes in temperature than yeasted dough, so keep an eye on it. If fermentation seems to have slowed to a crawl, it may be too cold. Relocate it to a warmer area and give it some time.

**Shape:** Turn the dough out onto a lightly floured work surface. Gently pat the dough out into a rough rectangle shape (10 by 15 inches/25 by 38 cm). Fold in the corners farthest from you as if you were folding in the sleeves of a T-shirt, then roll the dough up toward you like a yoga mat. Place it into a 9 by 5-inch (23 by 13 by 6 cm) loaf pan, seam side up, so it will open up in the oven.

**Proof:** Let the loaf proof, uncovered, at room temperature in the loaf pan for about an hour. A fully proofed loaf should rise above the edges of the pan and leave a soft impression when you press on it.

**Make a Steam Chamber:** Creating steam in the oven allows loaves to rise before the crust forms. Fill a sturdy metal tray or metal roasting pan (no ceramic or glass, please) halfway with water and place the pan on the lowest shelf of your oven. This will create steam as the oven preheats.

**Preheat:** Preheat the oven to 425°F (220°C).

**Bake:** Bake the loaf for 18 minutes, then open the oven to check on the loaf and let out the steam. Be cautious of the escaping steam and keep your face away from the door. Your loaf will open and split apart along the seam and should be a pale golden color. Bake for 15 minutes longer, or until it is a deep russet color.

**Cool:** Unmold the loaf from the pan right away and transfer to a wire rack to let cool for 30 minutes.

Sourdough loaves made with whole grain preserve a little better than yeasted breads. Store in a resealable plastic bag for up to 5 days.

 **baker's journal** Note the timing and results of your baking experience in your baker's notebook (see page 86). Repeat this loaf a few times to develop a rhythm and gain confidence with the sourdough process. Remember to evaluate your results according to aesthetics, crust, crumb, and flavor. Then you can compare this bake against your future bakes and other recipes and re-create your best results.

# Intermediate Dutch Oven Sourdough

Once you feel comfortable working with sourdough and making a simple tinned loaf, you can try using a Dutch oven. Dutch ovens deliver consistent heat, an enclosed steam environment, and professional-quality results in a home oven. It's hard to beat the crust created by this baking method. The confined steam helps higher-hydration loaves such as this one reach their full expression in the oven and creates a beautiful caramelization and sweetness in the final crust.

*Makes 1 loaf*

| INGREDIENT | WEIGHT | VOLUME |
|---|---|---|
| **For the Starter:** | | |
| All-purpose flour | 75 g | ½ cup plus 2 tablespoons |
| Water | 75 g | ¼ cup plus 1 tablespoon |
| **For the Dough:** | | |
| Water | 310 g | 1¼ cups |
| All-purpose flour | 300 g | 2½ cups |
| Whole wheat flour | 150 g | 1⅓ cups |
| Fine salt | 9 g | 1½ teaspoons |

**Feed and Scale the Starter:** Eight to 12 hours before mixing the dough, discard half of the starter (see page 198), then scale your starter to the amount needed in this recipe by feeding it with the amounts of flour and water indicated in the ingredients chart. Let the starter rise to its peak; it should double or triple in size in the container over the 8 to 12 hours.

**Prepare:** Weigh or measure all the ingredients and gather your supplies. Bring the water to the correct temperature, using the temperature chart (see page 27).

**Mix:** To make the dough, in a large bowl, combine the water and 135 grams (¾ cup) of sourdough starter. Use a spoon to mix gently until the starter is dispersed. (Set aside the remaining portion of the starter in its original container to retain your starter.) Add both flours and the salt. Mix by hand, using a grab-and-squish motion to thoroughly combine all the ingredients. The dough is well mixed when it is smooth and there are no dry bits of flour. This may take about 5 minutes.

**Rest:** Cover the bowl with a kitchen towel and let the dough rest for 15 minutes.

**Fold:** For this slightly higher-hydration dough, use the folding method to develop the gluten. Starting on the side of the bowl closest to you, scoop both hands under the sides of the dough and glide your hands around the perimeter of the bowl, each hand moving on one side in a semicircular motion, gently stretching the dough away from you as you go. Once your hands meet again at the top of the bowl, pull the dough over itself, across the bowl, back toward you. Work like this around the bowl until the dough forms a tight ball.

The stretching and folding organizes the proteins in the dough into strong weblike bonds that help the dough hold its structure throughout fermentation.

Folding develops the dough gently and works great for stickier doughs that would be hard to knead on a work surface. When kneading, we press against the work surface and fold the dough over itself. In the folding process, we re-create the same important motion of kneading—stretching the dough and folding it over, developing the gluten—but leaving the dough in the bowl can help prevent wetter doughs from getting stuck to the work surface.

**Rise:** Dust the dough with a bit of flour, cover with a kitchen towel (or plastic wrap, if necessary, in drier climates) and let rise for 3 hours. It should increase in size by roughly half. Leavened sourdough naturally rises at a slightly slower pace than yeasted doughs. You'll know the yeast is rising when the dough domes up slightly in the center and the surface has small bubbles all over it. Sourdough can be more sensitive to changes in temperature than yeasted dough, so keep an eye on it. If fermentation seems to have slowed to a crawl, it may be too cold. Relocate it to a warmer area and give it some time.

Remember to take notes so you have them for comparison to future loaves, and to evaluate the final loaf to help develop your skills.

**Shape:** Turn the dough out onto a lightly floured work surface, with the smooth top of the dough face down, leaving the underside facing up. Gently pat the dough out into a rough square shape. Fold the farthest edge of the dough in toward you, tacking it down in the middle of the dough. Then fold the near edge up to meet it in the middle, essentially performing a letter fold. Now turn the dough a quarter turn, and fold those edges the same way. You will end with a somewhat squared-off parcel. Turn this over and gently round the dough into a ball with your hands.

Special bread proofing baskets called bannetons or brotforms are typically made of cane or wicker and lined with linen. They are nice to have if you are a serious bread baker at this stage. Dust well with flour to prevent the dough from sticking to the linen, and then brush it out with a kitchen brush to maintain.

Dutch ovens get very hot and are quite heavy, so always use thick oven gloves, have a supervising adult nearby, and practice caution.

**Proof:** Use a banneton (a linen-lined basket made for proofing bread in) or a colander lined with a kitchen towel. Dust the linen or the towel and the loaf with a bit of whole wheat flour to prevent sticking. Place the dough in the basket or colander with the seam side down, resting on the towel. When you turn the loaf out to bake, it will be reversed with the seam side up. Let the loaf proof for 1 hour.

**Preheat:** Preheat the oven to 450°F (230°C) with the Dutch oven inside.

**Bake:** Unmold your loaf from its resting place onto a sheet of parchment paper. Using caution and good oven gloves, pick up the sides of the parchment like a hammock around the dough, and gently drop the proofed loaf into the Dutch oven, with the seam side up. Cover the Dutch oven with the lid.

Bake the loaf, covered, for 20 minutes, then open the oven to check on the loaf. Carefully remove the lid from the Dutch oven, being cautious of the escaping steam and keeping your face away from the pot. The loaf will have opened and split apart along the seam and should be a pale golden color. Bake for 10 to 15 minutes longer, or until it is a deep russet brown.

**Cool:** Use gloves to transfer the loaf from the Dutch oven to a wire rack and let cool for 30 minutes.

Crusty sourdough loaves stay fresh for a few days when simply placed cut side down on a cutting board. If you prefer very soft bread, slice it and store in a resealable plastic bag for up to a week. You can also freeze it. Pull out one slice at a time and pop straight into a toaster—it will taste freshly baked.

# Oatmeal or Multigrain Sourdough

You can infuse more nutrients into a loaf of bread by incorporating cooked whole grains, such as oat porridge, into the dough. Oats are a great source of fiber, antioxidants, and micronutrients, such as manganese, selenium, and phosphorus. Oat bread is delicious—it takes the heartiness and warmth of a bowl of oatmeal and transfers it to a piece of bread, to enjoy in a completely new way. It really shines toasted, spread with almond butter and a drizzle of honey on top.

*Makes 1 loaf*

| INGREDIENT | WEIGHT | VOLUME |
|---|---|---|
| **For the Starter:** | | |
| All-purpose flour | 60 g | ½ cup |
| Water | 60 g | ¼ cup |
| **For the Oat Porridge:** | | |
| Boiling water | 80 g | ⅓ cup |
| Rolled oats or multigrain hot cereal | 40 g, plus more to top the loaf | ⅓ cup plus 1 tablespoon |
| Salt | 2 g | ¼ teaspoon |
| **For the Dough:** | | |
| Water | 260 g | 1 cup plus 2 tablespoons |
| Whole wheat flour | 200 g | 1¾ cups |
| All-purpose flour | 200 g | 1⅓ cups |
| Fine salt | 9 g | 1½ teaspoons |

**Feed and Scale the Starter:** Eight to 12 hours before mixing the dough, discard half of the starter (see page 198), then scale your starter to the amount needed in this recipe by feeding it with the amounts of flour and water indicated in the ingredients chart. Let the starter rise to its peak; it should double or triple in size in the container over the 8 to 12 hours.

**Make the Oat Porridge:** In a large bowl, combine the boiling water, rolled oats (or multigrain hot cereal), and salt. Use a spoon to mix well. Set aside.

↑ There are many ways to add more delicious nutrition to a loaf of bread—brown rice, barley, or other cooked grains can be incorporated in the same way as the oats. Think about what you would like to have in your bread. You have all the building blocks; just keep the percentages and method the same and track your experiments!

**Prepare:** Weigh or measure all the ingredients and gather your supplies. Bring the water to the correct temperature, using the temperature chart (see page 27).

**Mix:** To make the dough, in a large bowl, combine the water and 120 grams (½ cup) of sourdough starter. Use a spoon to mix gently until the starter is dispersed. (Set aside the remaining portion of the starter in its original container to retain your starter.) Add both flours and the salt. Mix by hand, using a grab-and-squish motion to thoroughly combine all the ingredients. The dough is well mixed when it is smooth and there are no dry bits of flour. This may take about 5 minutes.

*continued*

**Rest:** Cover the bowl with a kitchen towel and let the dough rest for 15 minutes.

**Fold:** For this slightly higher-hydration dough, use the folding method to develop the gluten. First, add the reserved porridge. Using wet hands, spread the porridge all over the surface of the dough. Then, starting on the side of the bowl closest to you, scoop both hands under the sides of the dough and glide your hands around the perimeter of the bowl, each hand moving on one side in a semicircular motion, gently stretching the dough away from you as you go. Once your hands meet again at the top of the bowl, pull the dough over itself, across the bowl, back toward you. Work like this around the bowl until the dough forms a tight ball. If the dough feels tight or the oats are a bit dry, don't be afraid to wet your hands again and add small amounts of water to incorporate the porridge.

**Rise:** Dust the dough with a bit of flour, cover with a kitchen towel (or plastic wrap, if necessary, in drier climates), and let rise for 3 hours. It should increase in size by roughly half. Sometimes dough with porridge inside can rise faster than dough without an addition. You'll know the yeast is rising when the dough domes up slightly in the center and the surface has small bubbles all over it. Sourdough can be more sensitive to changes in temperature than yeasted dough, so keep an eye on it. If fermentation seems to have slowed to a crawl, it may be too cold. Relocate it to a warmer area and give it some time.

**Shape:** Turn the dough out onto a lightly floured work surface, with the smooth top of the dough face down, leaving the underside facing up. Gently pat the dough out into a rough square shape. Fold the farthest edge of the dough in toward you, tacking it down in the middle of the dough. Then fold the near edge up to meet it in the middle, essentially performing a letter fold. Now turn the dough a quarter turn, and fold those edges the same way. You will end with a somewhat squared-off

A good trick for testing when the rise is done is to cut off a portion of dough about the size of a strawberry and drop it in a glass of water. If it sinks, the dough may need another 30 minutes of fermentation time. If it floats, the dough has sufficient air from the fermentation.

You can use this method for other toppings, too, such as seeds. →

## is it nutritious?

Nutrition is the science and study of how food keeps humans healthy. Reading nutrition labels is a great life skill that can help you make good choices. Two important things we can look for are protein and fiber. These two nutrients are listed on labels and are usually a great combination to help us feel full for longer, give us energy, and enable good digestion. Try looking at the nutrition facts on the oats you used to make this bread, then compare it to a box of sweet cereal you have in your house or at the store. Do you think a piece of oat bread toast spread with peanut butter (a good mix of protein and fat) could improve your energy and mood stability over the day? What other foods can serve your body and mind this way?

parcel. Turn this over and gently round the dough into a ball with your hands.

**Coat the Dough:** To coat the outside of the loaf in oats, place a dampened towel on the counter, with a tray of dry uncooked oats next to it. Moisten the surface of the shaped loaf by rolling it around on the damp towel, then roll the surface of the loaf over the tray of oats.

**Proof:** Use a banneton (a linen-lined basket made for proofing bread in) or a colander lined with a kitchen towel. Dust the linen or the towel and the loaf with a bit of whole wheat flour to prevent sticking. Place the dough in the basket or colander with the seam side down, resting on the towel. When you turn the loaf out to bake, it will be reversed with the seam side up. Let the loaf proof for 1 hour.

**Preheat:** Preheat the oven to 450°F (230°C) with the Dutch oven inside.

**Bake:** Unmold your loaf from its resting place onto a sheet of parchment paper. Using caution and good oven gloves, pick up the sides of the parchment like a hammock around the dough, and gently drop the proofed loaf into the Dutch oven, with the seam side up. Cover the Dutch oven with the lid.

Bake the loaf, covered, for 20 minutes, then open the oven to check on the loaf. Carefully remove the lid from the Dutch oven, being cautious of the escaping steam and keeping your face away from the pot. The loaf will have opened and split apart along the seam and should be a pale golden color. Bake for 10 to 15 minutes longer, or until it is a deep russet brown.

**Cool:** Use gloves to transfer the loaf from the Dutch oven to a wire rack and let cool for 30 minutes.

Slice the bread and store it in a resealable plastic bag for up to 5 days to keep it soft.

# Sprouted Quinoa and Chia Sourdough

Sprouting is the process that kicks off the transition from a seed into a plant. This enzymatic process also breaks down starches to make them more digestible. Sprouting grains is a 3- to 4-day project. If you plan to bake on the weekend, for example, start the sprouting process at the beginning of the week. This bread is made with quinoa and chia seeds. Quinoa is easy to find in any grocery store and it's considered a superfood because it's high in protein and minerals, while chia seeds add an extra boost of protein, fiber, and vitamins. This bread is perfect for making avocado toast for breakfast or as a filling snack.

*Makes 1 loaf*

| INGREDIENT | WEIGHT | VOLUME |
|---|---|---|
| **For the Starter:** | | |
| All-purpose flour | 55 g | ½ cup |
| Water | 55 g | ¼ cup |
| **For the Dough:** | | |
| Water | 260 g | 1 cup plus 2 tablespoons |
| All-purpose flour | 200 g | 1⅔ cups |
| Whole wheat flour | 160 g | 1⅓ cups |
| Fine salt | 10 g | 1½ teaspoons |
| Sprouted red or white quinoa (see page 222) | 75 g | ⅔ cup |
| Chia seeds | 30 g | 3 rounded tablespoons |

**Feed and Scale the Starter:** Eight to 12 hours before mixing the dough, discard half of the starter (see page 198), then scale your starter to the amount needed in this recipe by feeding it with the amounts of flour and water indicated in the ingredients chart. Let the starter rise to its peak; it should double or triple in size in the container over the 8 to 12 hours.

**Prepare:** Weigh or measure all the ingredients and gather your supplies. Bring the water to the correct temperature, using the temperature chart (see page 27).

**Mix:** To make the dough, in a large bowl, combine the water and 110 grams (½ cup) of sourdough starter. Use a spoon to mix gently until the starter is dispersed. (Set aside the remaining portion of the starter in its original container to retain your starter.) Add both flours and the salt. Mix by hand, using a grab-and-squish motion to thoroughly combine all the ingredients. The dough is well mixed when it is smooth and there are no dry bits of flour. This may take about 5 minutes.

**Rest:** Cover the bowl with a kitchen towel and let the dough rest for 15 minutes.

continued

At first when incorporating quinoa and seeds it may feel like the dough is falling apart a bit. This is totally normal—it will come back together and strengthen as the fermentation continues. If you feel like it's a bit loose for your comfort, come back in 30 minutes and do a few more folds. It will tighten right up.

**Fold:** For this slightly higher-hydration dough, use the folding method to develop the gluten. First, add the quinoa and chia seeds. Using wet hands, spread them all over the surface of the dough. Then, starting on the side of the bowl closest to you, scoop both hands under the sides of the dough and glide your hands around the perimeter of the bowl, each hand moving on one side in a semicircular motion, gently stretching the dough away from you as you go. Once your hands meet again at the top of the bowl, pull the dough over itself, across the bowl, back toward you. Work like this around the bowl until the dough forms a tight ball. Don't be afraid to wet your hands again and add small amounts of water to incorporate the ingredients.

**Rise:** Dust the dough with a bit of flour, cover with a kitchen towel (or plastic wrap, if necessary, in drier climates), and let rise for 2½ to 3 hours. It should increase in size by roughly half. Leavened sourdough naturally rises at a slightly slower pace than yeasted doughs. You'll know the yeast is rising when the dough domes up slightly in the center and the surface has small bubbles all over it. Sourdough can be more sensitive to changes in temperature than yeasted dough, so keep an eye on it. If fermentation seems to have slowed to a crawl, it may be too cold. Relocate it to a warmer area and give it some time.

**Shape:** Turn the dough out onto a lightly floured work surface, with the smooth top of the dough face down, leaving the underside facing up. Gently pat the dough out into a rough square shape. Fold the farthest edge of the dough in toward you, tacking it down in the middle of the dough. Then fold the near edge up to meet it in the middle, essentially performing a letter fold. Now turn the dough a quarter turn, and fold those edges the same way. You will end with a somewhat squared-off parcel. Turn this over and gently round the dough into a ball with your hands.

This loaf already has seeds inside, but if you want to incorporate more seeds into the crust, sprinkle them in the banneton or on the towel and they will embed in the crust. You can use this technique for other breads, too.

**Proof:** Use a banneton (a linen-lined basket made for proofing bread in) or a colander lined with a kitchen towel. Dust the linen or the towel and the loaf with a bit of whole wheat flour to prevent sticking. Place the dough in the basket or colander with the seam side down, resting on the towel. When you turn the loaf out to bake, it will be reversed with the seam side up. Let the loaf proof for 1 hour.

**Preheat:** Preheat the oven to 450°F (230°C) with the Dutch oven inside.

**Bake:** Unmold your loaf from its resting place onto a sheet of parchment paper. Using caution and good oven gloves, pick up the sides of the parchment like a hammock around the dough, and gently drop the proofed loaf into the Dutch oven, with the seam side up. Cover the Dutch oven with the lid.

Bake the loaf, covered, for 20 minutes, then open the oven to check on the loaf. Carefully remove the lid from the Dutch oven, being cautious of the escaping steam and keeping your face away from the pot. The loaf will have opened and split apart along the seam and should be a pale golden color. Bake for 10 to 15 minutes longer, or until it is a deep russet brown.

**Cool:** Use gloves to transfer the loaf from the Dutch oven to a wire rack and let cool for 30 minutes.

Slice the bread and store it in a resealable plastic bag for up to 5 days to keep it soft.

# Sprouted Quinoa

Technically a seed, though classified as a whole grain, quinoa contains all the essential amino acids that make a complete protein. It's a good source of manganese, phosphorus, and copper and has an earthy, nutty flavor. The process of sprouting the quinoa, when the grain begins to open and become a plant, breaks down the starches of the grain so that its minerals and vitamins are more easily absorbed into our bodies.

Makes 1 cup (100 g) sprouted quinoa

| INGREDIENT | WEIGHT | VOLUME |
|---|---|---|
| Quinoa | 100 g | ½ cup plus 1 tablespoon |

Three to four days before you plan to bake, begin sprouting the quinoa.

**Day 1:** Place 100 grams (½ cup plus 1 tablespoon) of quinoa in a large mason jar and fill the jar with water. Soak the quinoa for 8 hours, then drain the water. Cover the mouth of the jar with a paper coffee filter and twist on the ring so it's secure but ventilated. Leave the quinoa in the jar overnight.

**Day 2:** Rinse the quinoa by filling the jar with water, giving it a shake or stir, then draining the water again by pouring it off. Cover with a coffee filter and ring and leave overnight.

**Day 3:** Repeat the rinsing process again by filling the jar with water, giving it a shake, then draining the water off. If the quinoa has sprouted, you will see little white threads emerging from the quinoa. If not, cover with a coffee filter and ring and leave the quinoa in the jar for another day.

**Day 4:** You should have a jar of sprouted quinoa by now. If you aren't ready to bake today, make sure the sprouts are dry, and store them in an airtight container in the fridge until you are ready. Sprouted grains can be stored for about 2 weeks. Sprouted quinoa is also great in salads or used to finish a soup.

 Sprouts (like fermentation) will happen faster at warm temperatures and slower at cool temperatures.

# Miche

A miche is a large sourdough loaf mainly made of whole wheat flour. It is a peasant loaf and similar to what bakers would have made in a shared community oven long ago. Its large size makes for a big canvas on which to practice scoring. Scoring is the act of cutting into the top of a loaf of bread with a knife, baker's lame (see page 228), or other sharp blade before it is baked. This is done for both functional and aesthetic reasons. The score on the top of a loaf can direct the opening of the loaf as it expands in the oven, as opposed to allowing the bread to come apart naturally at its seam. *Makes 1 large loaf*

| INGREDIENT | WEIGHT | VOLUME |
|---|---|---|
| **For the Starter:** | | |
| All-purpose flour | 200 g | 1⅔ cups |
| Water | 200 g | ⅞ cup |
| **For the Dough:** | | |
| Water | 350 g | 1½ cups plus 1 teaspoon |
| Honey (or any liquid sweetener you like) | 20 g | 1 tablespoon |
| Whole wheat flour | 320 g | 2¾ cups plus 2 tablespoons |
| All-purpose flour | 200 g | 1⅔ cups |
| Fine salt | 18 g | 1 tablespoon |

We are resting the dough without salt, a technique called autolyzing, which can be helpful for doughs that incorporate more whole-grain ingredients. It allows the dough to absorb the water and improves dough elasticity.

**Feed and Scale the Starter:** Eight to 12 hours before mixing the dough, discard half of the starter (see page 198), then scale your starter to the amount needed in this recipe by feeding it with the amounts of flour and water indicated in the ingredients chart. Let the starter rise to its peak; it should double or triple in size in the container over the 8 to 12 hours.

**Prepare:** Weigh or measure all the ingredients and gather your supplies. Bring the water to the correct temperature, using the temperature chart (see page 27).

**Mix:** To make the dough, in a large bowl, combine the water, honey, and 400 grams (2⅔ cups) of sourdough starter. Use a spoon to mix gently until the starter is dispersed. (Set aside the remaining portion of the starter in its original container to retain your starter.) Add both flours. Mix by hand, using a grab-and-squish motion to thoroughly combine all the ingredients. The dough is well mixed when it is smooth and there are no dry bits of flour. This may take about 5 minutes.

**Rest:** Cover the bowl with a kitchen towel and let the dough rest for 30 minutes.

continued

**Fold:** Scatter the salt over the dough, incorporating it well with wet hands and using small amounts of water on your hands to work the salt into the dough. For this slightly higher-hydration dough, use the folding method to develop the gluten. Starting on the side of the bowl closest to you, scoop both hands under the sides of the dough and glide your hands around the perimeter of the bowl, each hand moving on one side in a semicircular motion, gently stretching the dough away from you as you go. Once your hands meet again at the top of the bowl, pull the dough over itself, across the bowl, back toward you. Work like this around the bowl until the dough forms a tight ball.

**Rise:** Dust the dough with a bit of flour, cover with a kitchen towel (or plastic wrap, if necessary, in drier climates), and let rise for 3 hours, folding the dough a second time after 1 hour. It should increase in size by roughly half. Leavened sourdough naturally rises at a slightly slower pace than yeasted doughs. You'll know the yeast is rising when the dough domes up slightly in the center and the surface has small bubbles all over it. Sourdough can be more sensitive to changes in temperature than yeasted dough, so keep an eye on it. If fermentation seems to have slowed to a crawl, it may be too cold. Relocate it to a warmer area and give it some time.

**Shape:** Turn the dough out onto a lightly floured work surface, with the smooth top of the dough face down, leaving the underside facing up. Fold the farthest edge of the dough in toward you, tacking it down in the middle of the dough. Then fold the near edge up to meet it in the middle, essentially performing a letter fold. Now turn the dough a quarter turn, and fold those edges the same way. You will end with a somewhat squared-off parcel. Turn this over and gently round the dough into a ball with your hands.

**Proof:** Use a very large banneton (a linen-lined basket made for proofing bread in) or a colander lined with a kitchen towel. Dust the linen or kitchen towel and the loaf with a bit of whole wheat flour to prevent sticking. Place the dough in the basket or colander with the seam side up. Let the loaf proof for 1 hour.

**Make a Steam Chamber:** Fill a sturdy metal tray or metal roasting pan (no ceramic or glass, please) halfway with water and place the pan on the lowest shelf of your oven. This will create steam as the oven preheats.

**Preheat:** This large loaf won't quite fit in a Dutch oven, so we'll bake it on a pizza stone. (You can use a baking sheet if you don't have a pizza stone.) Place a pizza stone on the middle shelf in the oven while it preheats to 450°F (230°C).

**Bake:** Unmold your loaf from its resting place onto a floured pizza peel or cutting board. Using a baker's lame, carve your baker's mark into the top of the loaf with a quick and decisive slashing motion. If you aren't sure where to start, try a simple, big, bold X right through the middle.

If you're struggling with scoring, try placing your loaf in the fridge for 20 to 30 minutes while you preheat the oven; this will make the dough a little firmer and easier to score.

The key to scoring bread is to be assertive. Hesitation can lead to dragging on the blade, which can prevent you from getting a nice deep cut into the loaf. You can be more decorative when you get more confident, but start with bold straight lines (like an X or a square)—these are the easiest way to get those strong forceful strokes with the blade across the soft dough.

Carefully slide the loaf onto the pizza stone and bake for 20 minutes. After 20 minutes, carefully remove the tray of water and bake the loaf for 15 to 20 minutes longer, or until it is a beautiful dark brown all over.

continued

**Cool:** Use gloves to transfer the loaf from the oven to a wire rack to let cool. This larger loaf may take 45 minutes to an hour to cool.

This loaf has a lot of whole wheat and a high portion of sourdough, so it will keep and age very well. Wrap the loaf in a large kitchen towel to keep it fresh longer. You can also cut it into fourths, which can be stored in resealable plastic bags for longer storage.

## master bread scoring

Scoring the bread means carving a baker's mark into the top of a loaf of bread. When community ovens were common, a baker's mark on top of a loaf indicated that the bread came from a certain bakery or person. You can score your bread with a lame (pronounced "lom"), which is a razor blade in a sticklike holder. Teens may have some experience using a razor for shaving, an X-Acto blade for art projects, a knife in the kitchen, or a box cutter at work. Use the same caution when using a lame—hold only the handle, and be careful when changing the blade. Try designing your mark on paper first. You can look at the bread of other bakeries online for inspiration.

## Parting words to a child who has grown up baking through this book:

We have come a long way! We engaged all five senses getting to know the craft of bread, baked with the seasons and locally grown produce, traced bread back through history and across the globe, and took bread apart and put it back together with math and science. Now that you've become a skilled bread baker, it's something you can hone for life. Baking bread takes patience, conscientiousness, consideration, and thoughtfulness. Calling yourself a bread baker means contributing to a space of goodwill, generosity, sharing, and collaboration. The camaraderie of the bread baking community is special and welcoming to hobbyists, beginners, and professionals alike. A good baker's ethos should include caring for neighbors (bake extra and share), supporting the community (shop small and local and at farmers' markets), being a good steward of resources (be thoughtful and sustainable wherever you can), pushing environmental progress forward (seek out and buy flour from local mills and grain from local farms when you are able, even if it's only a little bit at a time), and nurturing those who look up to you (share your starter, your skills, your advice, and your tips with new bakers). Bake sales are always a great way to contribute to a cause that you care about. If help is needed somewhere, the local baker will typically be there. Studies show that what makes people most happy in life doesn't tend to be accolades or monetary success but a sense of purpose and service while doing something that they enjoy. This is the way bakers make their indelible mark on the world, and it's time for you to make yours in whatever big or small way you can! I will always be here, cheering for you, your success, and, most important, your deepest contentment.

—Bonnie

# Resources

Most people do not live in big cities and may have trouble finding specialized baking tools. A lot of good basics can be found affordably at a restaurant supply store; simply do an online search for your area using the terms "restaurant supply" and "small wares," which is what restaurant folks call all their general tools. Big metal mixing bowls, piles of half-sheet pans, pizza cutters, dough cutters and scrapers, food-safe plastic containers—all these things are affordable at a restaurant supply store and better quality than what you'll find at big-box stores.

For more specific baking items, this is where Amazon excels. I have a linked materials list for you on my website with everything needed to bake well, from thermometers and scales and rolling pins right down to the parchment paper and beeswax wraps. Visit my website at:

**alchemybread.com/book**

For online baking video classes that break down into further details every technique in this book and my previous book for beginners, visit my website:

**alchemybread.com/classes**

For all kinds of baking recipes, high-quality content, and tutorials, I love the King Arthur baking website:

**kingarthurbaking.com**

For sourdough-specific guidance that is incredibly detailed and focused, I highly recommend my friend Maurizio Leo's website:

**theperfectloaf.com**

All the aprons pictured in this book are handmade from organic and sustainable hemp by Charlie Pennes of Whitebark Workwear in Los Angeles. Remember, your clothing and food are grown in the same soil.

**whitebarkworkwear.com**

# Further Reading

Some books I enjoyed reading while writing this book:

## Enriched Breads for Beginners

*Simplicity Parenting: Using the Extraordinary Power of Less to Raise Calmer, Happier, and More Secure Kids* by Kim John Payne and Lisa M. Ross

*The Brave Learner: Finding Everyday Magic in Homeschool, Learning, and Life* by Julie Bogart

*Beyond the Rainbow Bridge: Nurturing Our Children from Birth to Seven* by Barbara J. Patterson (author), Pamela Bradley (author), and Jean Riordan (illustrator)

## Seasonal Breads

*Edible Schoolyard* by Alice Waters

*Sunflower Houses: Garden Discoveries for Children of All Ages* by Sharon Lovejoy

## Breads Around the World

*Six Thousand Years of Bread: Its Holy and Unholy History* by H. E. Jacob

*Nectar and Ambrosia: An Encyclopedia of Food in World Mythology* by Tamra Andrews

*Cooked: A Natural History of Transformation* by Michael Pollan

## Sourdough Breads

*Culinary Reactions: The Everyday Chemistry of Cooking* by Simon Quellen Field

*How to Bake Pi: An Edible Exploration of the Mathematics of Mathematics* by Eugenia Cheng

*Bread Lab!* by Kim Binczewski

# Acknowledgments

This book was written almost entirely during the coronavirus pandemic of 2020–2022. It's hard to overstate the challenge of parenting, homeschooling, and working from home during this time while mostly separated from our extended family, friends, and community for such a strange and extended period.

First, I must thank my kids. To my eldest, Sophie: I am so proud of you. You are a kind and empathetic and loving person and an amazing friend to all your friends—and mine, too. Thank you for all the trips to the bookstore and library, sweet doodles in the margins of my notebooks, and thoughtful feedback on my writing as you grow into an incredible writer and talented artist yourself. Watching your art style progress is so inspiring. Thank you for letting me trade boba tea dates for babysitting your siblings when I needed to work. I love sharing your dark humor, watching and analyzing movies with you, hearing about the books you are reading, and listening to your incredible Spotify playlists. When we sit on the couch or bed together listening to music, both wrapped up in our own books, writing or drawing, I feel so content.

Gabriel: I have loved working alongside you and watching your love of baking develop into a true passion over the past few years. You are so analytical and insightful; I love your intense lines of questioning. Thank you for the support you give when you are in the bakery checking my timers and looking over my product. You always give sharp and uncompromising feedback, and I love that about you. I appreciate your appetite for learning new skills and tinkering with things like origami. I loved watching you learn to use an espresso machine this year, all the fantastic lattes we made together, and all the times we had tea and played a board game at the end of a long bake day. I cherish the time teaching you knife skills and seeing you take pride in them, and talking about your dreams in the early-morning kitchen. I love going to the farmers' market with you to be extra selective about the fruit, and planting things in our garden and watching them grow. Working side by side and making plans is our happy place.

Leo, my sweetheart: I have loved watching you work with your hands, whether it's kneading dough, putting sauce and cheese on pizza, or eating all the cheese, pieces of butter, fistfuls of sugar, and random pieces of raw dough you can get your hands on. You have a zest for life (and sweets) that is unmatched. You are always close to me for a hug or a snuggle or a kiss, and your laugh is one of my favorite sounds. I can't make cookies or pastries without hearing you behind me waiting for a chocolate chip or to help clean the giant mixer paddle. Thanks for always reminding me to be in the joyous sensory moment and to live through my hands and taste buds while laughing. Holding you in my arms is the best place to be.

Thank you, Jennifer Kara, for all the long walks, cups of tea, and long talks. You have graciously taken me under your wing and shown me so much about how to be a mother, how to be human, and how to be a matriarch in a community. These past two years you taught me so much about how to stand up for myself, ask for what I need, and stay strong when I really needed it.

I'd like to thank my dearest homeschooling compatriots, Janelle Shank and Kristi Mazuelos (and their kids), for forming a little pod with us and joining us in weekly swimming or trampoline jumping to keep our young people's sanity intact, and for commiserating through the shared trials of our kids having their social lives mostly paused. Thank you for taking my kids to various activities as things opened again so I could steal a day of writing, and for checking on me and listening to me through some tough times, and for your heartfelt stewardship of our children's hearts. Also, thanks for lending me your kids for the photo shoot!

Thanks to my friends Candace Jenkins, Jenny Winzey, and Michelle Adams for letting me dump my exhausted self into a corner of their lovely child-free home environments to hole up with my laptop and work in stolen quiet moments. Thanks for all the best snacks, funny memes, sanity-saving picnics, long walks, and even longer phone calls. I love you.

Thank you to Karina Jauregui and Emily Cowdrey, my favorite cooking and teaching companions. Emily, thank you for adding your cooking instructor feedback, letting me rifle through all your books, and keeping the food flowing with spontaneity and fun. Kari, thanks for sharing your pure joy in the artistic and colorful qualities of food as art. I am always inspired to make things more beautiful and more delicious when I am working beside you. Also, I couldn't have made it through the photo shoot without all your help.

Thanks to Marilyn Diaz and Patrick Norris for the support in making initial photos for the proposal for this book and for helping craft the creative vision of what this book would be. I am so inspired by both of you, and I love collaborating with you. I love sharing food, space, and work with you so much. Talking through our visions for the future is so precious.

Thank you, Ashley Lima, for designing the proposal for this book, for all the extra support and friendship that was so far above and beyond what I expected, and for the photography and styling of this book. I can't say how grateful I am that you arrived in my life at exactly the right time, like an angel. Thanks to Judy Pray and Bella Lemos at Artisan Books for patiently editing this book and shaping the organization of the ideas and concepts, and deep appreciation for my amazing agent, Rica Allanic.

Thank you to my local Alchemy Bread community, which includes too many special people to name individually but is made up of all those who hold up our town and our creative communities, and who feed and teach our friends and neighbors. I appreciate you not only for your continued patronage of my tiny business and support of me personally but for everything that you do for our community at large. I see you making the world a better place day by day. We do have the kindest and most generous people at work in our sacred circle, and I am living with my gratitude for you in my heart every single day.

Thank you to my community of colleagues in the baking and food world, who are too many to list. I couldn't have been luckier in life to have some of the most down-to-earth, solid, and loving people as friends and respected peers and mentors in the craft of bread. I appreciate every single one of you who has held on to me and lifted me up. I love our reciprocal, kind, and loving group committed to creating a better world. I especially need to thank beautiful and inspiring Sarah C. Owens for introducing me to my agent, Rica Allanic. (My hero. Thank you.) The rambunctious Martin Philip, who is a legendary writer and baker and generously helpful mentor, resource, and cheerleader. (Thanks, bread dad!) Alexandra Allen, the perfectionist Virgo who tested many of these recipes with me and is the best hype woman anyone could ever ask for, thank you for relentlessly encouraging me and never letting up. Ryan Mondragon, thanks for teaching me how to make better pizza, showing up with melon for the kids on hot days, bringing me a ginger smoothie when I lost my voice halfway through the photo shoot, and being a supportive friend in so many small practical ways. Eli Coleman, thanks for being the most beautiful hand model, but even more importantly for bringing so much laughter and joy into our home.

Thank you to my readers and supporters of my first book and this one—there are so many of you! I love seeing your bakes when you tag me on Instagram, I love hearing your stories of how you connect with others through your bread, I love hearing about your journey to make great bread, and I've even enjoyed meeting a lot of you in person and hope to meet many more of you! Thank you for making my first book a success so I could get a chance to make this one. I hope it serves you and your family well for many years and that you make a lot of special memories with these recipes. My favorite thing in the world is seeing you guys baking with and for your kids, families, neighbors, and friends. You can always connect with me on Instagram. I'm proud of you.

Love,
Your bread mom

# Index

Page numbers in *italics* refer to recipe photos.

# Conversion Charts

For accurate results when baking bread, it's important to refer to the specific metric weights in each recipe. For reference or general cooking, here are rounded-off equivalents between the metric system and the traditional systems that are used in the United States to measure weight and volume.

| WEIGHTS | | VOLUME | | |
|---|---|---|---|---|
| **US/UK** | **Metric** | **American** | **Imperial** | **Metric** |
| 1 oz | 30 g | ¼ tsp | | 1.25 ml |
| 2 oz | 55 g | ½ tsp | | 2.5 ml |
| 3 oz | 85 g | 1 tsp | | 5 ml |
| 4 oz (¼ lb) | 115 g | ½ Tbsp (1½ tsp) | | 7.5 ml |
| 5 oz | 140 g | 1 Tbsp (3 tsp) | | 15 ml |
| 6 oz | 170 g | ¼ cup (4 Tbsp) | 2 fl oz | 60 ml |
| 7 oz | 200 g | ⅓ cup (5 Tbsp) | 2½ fl oz | 75 ml |
| 8 oz (½ lb) | 225 g | ½ cup (8 Tbsp) | 4 fl oz | 125 ml |
| 9 oz | 255 g | ⅔ cup (10 Tbsp) | 5 fl oz | 150 ml |
| 10 oz | 285 g | ¾ cup (12 Tbsp) | 6 fl oz | 175 ml |
| 11 oz | 310 g | 1 cup (16 Tbsp) | 8 fl oz | 250 ml |
| 12 oz | 340 g | 1¼ cups | 10 fl oz | 300 ml |
| 13 oz | 370 g | 1½ cups | 12 fl oz | 350 ml |
| 14 oz | 395 g | 2 cups (1 pint) | 16 fl oz | 500 ml |
| 15 oz | 425 g | 2½ cups | 20 fl oz (1 pint) | 625 ml |
| 16 oz (1 lb) | 455 g | 5 cups | 40 fl oz (1 qt) | 1.25 l |

| OVEN TEMPERATURES | | | |
|---|---|---|---|
| | **°F** | **°C** | **Gas Mark** |
| very cool | 250–275 | 130–140 | ½–1 |
| cool | 300 | 148 | 2 |
| warm | 325 | 163 | 3 |
| moderate | 350 | 177 | 4 |
| moderately hot | 375–400 | 190–204 | 5–6 |
| hot | 425 | 218 | 7 |
| very hot | 450–475 | 232–245 | 8–9 |

## About the Author

Bonnie Ohara is the owner of a small cottage bakery called Alchemy Bread and a mom of three. When she's not baking or teaching other people to bake, you can find her picking out produce at the farmers' market, checking out picture books and cookbooks alike from the local library, or making dinner with her friends.